NATHANIEL HARRIS

Great Masters of World Painting

Botticelli
Canaletto · Watteau
Cézanne
Titian

SPRING
BOOKS

London New York Sydney Toronto

© Copyright 1974 by
The Hamlyn Publishing Group Limited
London · New York · Sydney · Toronto
Astronaut House, Feltham, Middlesex, England
ISBN 0 600 33976 9
First published 1974
Printed in Italy
by Arnoldo Mondadori Editore
Officine Grafiche - Verona

Botticelli

Sandro Botticelli, one of the greatest Italian painters, was born at Florence in or around 1445; we can work out the date fairly accurately from information given to the tax collector by Botticelli's father, Mariano Filipepi. Mariano was a tanner, but he seems to have apprenticed young Sandro—properly called Alessandro Filipepi—to a goldsmith. It was from the goldsmith—or according to another story from his brother—that Sandro acquired the nickname Botticelli ('little barrel').

Later still, Botticelli persuaded his father that he was more suited to be a painter, and so he was apprenticed to a well known master, Fra Filippo Lippi. There was nothing unusual about this, for painting was still looked on as a craft to be studied under a qualified practitioner, When the gifted apprentice became a master in his turn, he opened a workshop and took on apprentices to help him prepare his materials and perhaps, as they progressed, to do some of the painting. In this way a successful master could make his workshop into a miniature factory, turning out quantities of commissioned Madonnas or Adorations. This was the pattern of Botticelli's career in the 1470s. He became a respected master with his own workshop and apprentices, the most renowned of whom was Filippino Lippi, the son of his old teacher.

Botticelli is one of the most distinctive of all painters, with a personal, poetic style that must surely have been the expression of an unusual temperament. The most striking thing about his works is their lyrical, melancholy atmosphere. Botticelli's art is not one of human involvement. It is reflective and detached; whatever their gestures indicate to the contrary, his figures are essentially isolated, as if absorbed in acting out hieratic roles in a ritual drama. The atmosphere is reinforced by Botticelli's superb sense of design, and above all by his employment of strong, fluent lines to define and model his forms. He makes little use of varying shades of colour to create three-dimensional modelling, and even less use of effects of light and shade. The famous *Birth of Venus* (plate 32), for example, might almost be called a coloured drawing; colour is an important element in it because it heightens the tender, magical atmosphere, but it is quite possible to imagine the picture without it. The opposition between drawing and colour, between line and tone, was to have a long history in painting. The Florentine school had always been based on drawing, and in this respect Botticelli can be considered the supreme exponent of his city's tradition.

Botticelli was evidently one of those artists who find themselves early in life. True, the Madonnas he painted as a young man (plates 1, 2) are uncharacteristically warm and partly modelled with subtle tones; but *Fortitude* (plate 3) already has the long body and remote air of figures in the mature Botticelli's work. Even more striking is *Judith* (plate 5), in which the mood of the painting is (as so often with Botticelli) completely at variance with its subject matter—in this case the triumphal return of a Biblical virago who has just cut off the head of an enemy general. Judith is a type that is to recur again and again in Botticelli's paintings, whether as Madonna or Venus: an idealised, girlish figure, inaccessible and sad. Despite the bloody sword in her hand and the soldiers in the landscape background, it comes as a shock to realise that the maidservant is not stepping out with the laundry but carrying the severed head of Holofernes.

Within a few years Botticelli had the most powerful family in Florence as his patrons. The city was nominally a republic, but since 1434 the great banking family of Medici had acquired a near-absolute authority which was passed on from Cosimo to Piero de' Medici, and from Piero to his son Lorenzo. Lorenzo de' Medici, soon known as Lorenzo the Magnificent, ruled Florence from 1469 to his death in 1492. His prestige was enormous; he treated as an equal with kings and popes, and gave Florence a European status out of all proportion to her real strength. He also gathered about him the outstanding poets and philosophers of the day, men such as Marsilio Ficino and Angelo Poliziano who were inspired by the literature and ideals of ancient Greece and Rome. At Lorenzo's villa in the Tuscan countryside he and his friends feasted and philosophised. Their thoughts, and the art they patronised, were one of the glories of the great age of the Italian Renaissance.

It is hard to know how closely Botticelli was associated with this charmed circle. The chief authority for Botticelli's life is Giorgio Vasari, whose *Lives of the Most Excellent Painters* was published in 1550, a good many years after the events they relate. According to Vasari, the three kings in one of Botticelli's versions of the *Adoration of the Magi* (plate 9) are portraits of members of the Medici family. (The figure on the far right, gazing straight at us over his shoulder, is said to be Botticelli's self-portrait.) He also painted a portrait of Lorenzo's younger brother, Giuliano (plate 14), and designed

Giuliano's standard for a tournament held in 1475. Finally, in 1478 Botticelli painted a fresco (destroyed a few years later) which featured the hanging of the conspirators who had attacked Lorenzo and Giuliano in Florence Cathedral, killing Giuliano.

The exact nature of the Medici connection is of interest because Botticelli painted the most famous and perhaps the most enigmatic of his pictures for the family: the *Primavera* ('Spring'; plates 18–20), *The Birth of Venus* (plate 32), and *Venus and Mars* (plates 33, 34). Here the freedom and boldness of Botticelli's line reach a culmination, while the soft browns, greens and yellows unite the gods and goddesses with the natural world and accentuate the quiet lyricism of the mood. Paintings that clearly belong to this group, though far less well known, are *Pallas and the Centaur* (plate 26) and the Villa Lemmi frescos (plates 29, 30).

On one level these are straightforward mythological pictures, typical of the revivalistic zeal of the Renaissance, in which everything to do with Greece and Rome was worshipped. In the *Primavera*, Venus, goddess of love, is surrounded by Flora (goddess of flowers), the three Graces and the god Mercury. The scene on the far right is confusing in that it really takes place *before* the 'action' in the rest of the painting: Zephyr is capturing the nymph Chloris, who is thereby being changed into Flora. In *The Birth of Venus* the goddess emerges from the waves as in the classical myth. And in *Mars and Venus* the god of war sleeps, presumably exhausted by his encounter with Venus, while Pan-like children play with his helmet and lance.

The trouble with this interpretation is that the

whole atmosphere of the paintings is markedly unclassical. In particular, Venus is not the lusty lady of mythology but a sublimely innocent being who radiates tenderness. Of course this may have been a result of ignorance or misinterpretation on the part of Botticelli; but a more plausible explanation is that the painter was trying to give visual expression to the Neoplatonic philosophy of Lorenzo's circle. Neoplatonism was a set of doctrines originating in Antiquity, when the ideas of the Greek philosopher Plato had been reinterpreted in mystical terms. Lorenzo and his friends mixed in Christian and Renaissance concepts to create a philosophy in which Greek and Roman mythology, Christianity and a cult of beauty could be reconciled. In this, the ancient gods were not rivals of Jesus but symbolic entities. Venus, for example, came to represent love in all its aspects, spiritual as well as physical, and even the entire range of admirable worldly qualities. Having created these allegorical personages, the Neoplatonists made them the subject of an obscure impassioned poetry. In effect they invented a new mythology which—if this interpretation is correct—was translated into paint by Botticelli. This would indicate that there is a 'lost' meaning underlying the literal meaning of each painting. The explanation is the more attractive because we do sense a mystery in these pictures—the presence of a weight of emotion that seems hardly justified by the subject matter. And though we might not be much enlightened if we were certain that *Venus and Mars* represented the triumph of the humane virtues over the spirit of discord, a Neoplatonic key might clarify the situation in *Pallas and the Centaur* and explain the exact nature of the relationships in the *Primavera*.

Another link between Botticelli and the Medici circle was their common passion for the works of the great 14th-century poet Dante Alighieri. Botticelli is said to have written a commentary on Dante's *Divine Comedy*, and he certainly made a series of drawings to illustrate the poem. He is also the likely author of the 'portrait' in plate 25.

In 1481–82 Botticelli was in Rome. He was summoned there by the Borgia pope Sixtus IV, who was already employing some of Italy's most famous artists to decorate the chapel of his palace, the Sistine. In time the Sistine Chapel became one of the great showpieces of Italian art, with paintings by Ghirlandaio, Perugino, Signorelli, Pinturicchio, Piero di Cosimo, and finally Michelangelo, whose years of work on the chapel ceiling have passed into legend. Botticelli's contributions (plates 21–24) are not the most impressive of his works; both the grandiose atmosphere of 16th-century Rome and the scale on which he was expected to work must have been uncongenial to his temperament. Two features of these frescos are worth remarking. Each consists not of one but of several scenes. In *The Destruction of Korah*, for example, we can read off the story from right to left: the stoning of Moses by rebels against his authority; their discomfiture; and the earth opening to swallow them up. This 'continuous representation' had been quite a common device but was beginning to die out as greater realism became fashionable. The second feature is the use of real Roman backgrounds—Sixtus IV's Hospital of San Spirito in the *Purification* and the Arch of Constantine in the *Destruction*. This, like the portrayal of Biblical figures in Renaissance dress, had long been standard practice.

Botticelli's style changed considerably in his later years, almost certainly because he passed through some kind of religious crisis. According to Vasari, the painter became a follower of Fra Girolamo Savonarola, a puritanical reforming monk who was the virtual ruler of Florence between 1494 and 1498. Savonarola was a preacher of burning eloquence whose wild visions of death and judgement terrified his congregations. His condemnations of worldliness led to a 'Bonfire of Vanities' in which carnival masks, cosmetics, books of verse, playing cards and paintings were committed to the flames while the people danced around in joy. Doubtless a good many of Botticelli's pictures were on the pile. His loyalty to Savonarola led him to give up painting, a fact that accounts for the poverty and obscurity of his later years.

So says Vasari. He is certainly wrong about Botticelli giving up painting, since a number of pictures have survived that date from several years after Savonarola's death. Furthermore in 1498, when the monk fell from power and was burnt in the marketplace, Botticelli stayed in Florence although many disciples of Savonarola slipped out of the city in fear of their lives. So it seems unlikely that Botticelli was fully committed to Savonarola's cause. On the other hand one of Botticelli's later paintings, *The Mystic Crucifixion* (plate 48), is thoroughly in the spirit of Savonarola as well as containing symbols used by the preacher such as the otherwise inexplicable red crosses hovering around the figure of Jesus. This is a threatening, apocalyptic vision. The Magdalen, sorrowful and repentant, clings to the cross. An angel beats an obviously symbolic animal. And in the background lies not Jerusalem but the city of Florence, about to be engulfed for her sins.

Whatever his exact relationship to Savonarola, Botticelli was clearly a troubled man. He was, besides, living in troubled times. The death of Lorenzo the Magnificent in 1492 marked the end of Florence's golden age, politically even more than culturally. Botticelli's patrons, the Medici, were expelled from Florence. The French invaded Italy, initiating a new era of foreign interventions and occupations that the divided Italians were powerless to resist. And, rising and falling terribly against the background of these events, Savonarola prophesied doom and destruction.

None of this appears directly in Botticelli's paintings (apart from *The Mystic Crucifixion*) but the sense of disturbance in them is unmistakeable. For a time his Madonnas grow still more remote, giving an impression of complete alienation (plates 35, 36). The postures of his figures become exaggerated and their gestures wild and sweeping. In the *Annunciation* (plate 38) the effect is graceful and balletic, but elsewhere (plates 11, 41–44) it is often violent and over-emphatic, as if the painter were trying to work himself up into a feeling of intensity that did not come naturally to him. A climax is reached in two extraordinary *pietàs* (plates 45, 46) where the brilliant metallic colours, hieratic poses and masterly composition create an overwhelming impression. Plate 45 in particular, with its tight grouping and daring placing of the mourners' heads, has a unique sinister grandeur.

The narrative and allegorical paintings, with

their grandiose backgrounds of pseudo-Roman architecture, require a few words of explanation. In *The Calumny of Apelles* (plate 41), Hate, Ignorance, Suspicion, Calumny (in the blue robe) and her handmaidens are crowding in on the king to malign the young man being drawn along by his hair. The figures on the left are Truth (naked – of course) and Penitence. It is a strange picture, energised by the toppling figure of the handmaiden in the red robe. *Lucretia* (plate 43) is the well known story of the Roman matron who was raped by King Tarquin, killed herself, and so prompted Brutus to lead the revolt that made ancient Rome a republic. *Virginia* (plate 42) has a very similar plot, but in this the girl is claimed as a slave and killed by her own father to prevent her being dishonoured; he then raises the army against the tyranny of the decemvirs. St Zenobius (plate 44) is curing various afflictions. A notable feature of all these paintings is the grandiose, imaginary, Roman-style architecture in the backgrounds.

As if to show that a great painter will always escape definition, the little *Last Communion of St Jerome* (plate 47) has a seriousness and compassionate sense of involvement that is rare at any period of Botticelli's career. By contrast, the famous *Mystic Nativity* (plate 49) seems a partial return to Botticelli's earlier style, with a sad, still Nativity, albeit fringed with rather unconvincing rejoicing angels and discomfited demons.

From Botticelli's last years we have the uncharacteristic *Agony in the Garden* (plate 50), which may represent an effort to paint in a more fashionable style. There is certainly evidence that after about 1500 Botticelli was glad to accept commissions that other painters had turned down. But he was still eminent enough to sit on the committee responsible for deciding the site of Michelangelo's gigantic statue of David. Vasari says that Botticelli had no sense of the value of money, and that he died old, poor and decrepit at the age of seventy-eight. As he got Botticelli's age wrong (he died in 1510, at sixty five) we can hope that he was wrong about the rest, and that the painter was admired and respected to the end.

THE PLATES

1 *Madonna and Child. c.* 1468–70. Panel. $28\frac{3}{8} \times 20\frac{1}{2}$ in. (72 × 52 cm.). Louvre, Paris.

2 *Madonna of the Rose Bush. c.* 1469–70. Panel. $49 \times 25\frac{1}{4}$ in. (124 × 64 cm.). Uffizi, Florence.

3 *Fortitude.* 1470. Panel. 65 × 34 in. (167 × 87 cm.). Uffizi, Florence.

4 *Madonna with St Cosmas, St Damian and Other Saints. c.* 1470–72. Panel. $67 \times 76\frac{1}{2}$ in. (170 × 194 cm.). Uffizi, Florence.

5 *Judith with the Head of Holofernes. c.* 1470–72. Panel. $12\frac{1}{2} \times 9$ in. (31 × 25 cm.). Uffizi, Florence.

6 *Discovery of the Murder of Holofernes. c.* 1470–72. Panel. $12\frac{1}{2} \times 9$ in. (31 × 25 cm.). Uffizi, Florence.

7 *Madonna of the Eucharist. c.* 1472. Panel. $33 \times 24\frac{3}{4}$ in. (84 × 65 cm.). Isabella Stewart Gardner Museum, Boston.

8 *Adoration of the Magi. c.* 1472–76. Panel. Diameter $51\frac{1}{2}$ in. (131.5 cm.). National Gallery, London.

9 *Adoration of the Magi. c.* 1476–77. Panel. $43\frac{1}{2} \times 52\frac{3}{4}$ in. (111 × 134 cm.). Uffizi, Florence.

10 *Adoration of the Magi. c.* 1481–82. Panel. 28 × 41 in. (71 × 104 cm.). National Gallery of Art, Washington D.C.

11 *Adoration of the Magi.* c. 1500. Panel. $42\frac{1}{4} \times 68\frac{1}{8}$ in. (107.5 × 173 cm.). Uffizi, Florence.

12 *Portrait of a Man with a Medal.* c. 1473–74. Panel. $23 \times 17\frac{1}{4}$ in. (57.5 × 44 cm.). Uffizi, Florence.

13 *St Sebastian.* c. 1474. Panel. $76\frac{3}{4} \times 29\frac{1}{2}$ in. (195 × 75 cm.). Staatliche Museen, Gemäldegalerie, Berlin-Dahlem.

14 *Portrait of Giuliano de' Medici.* c. 1475. Panel. $21\frac{1}{2} \times 14\frac{1}{4}$ in. (54.5 × 36.5 cm.). Crespi Collection, Milan.

15 *Portrait of a Lady, traditionally Smeralda Bandinelli.* c. 1471–78. $25\frac{1}{2} \times 16\frac{1}{8}$ in. (66 × 41 cm.). Victoria & Albert Museum, London.

16 *Portrait of a Young Woman.* c. 1478. Panel. $24 \times 15\frac{3}{4}$ in. (61 × 40 cm.). Palazzo Pitti, Florence.

17 *St Augustine.* c. 1480. Fresco. $60 \times 44\frac{1}{8}$ in. (152 × 112 cm.). Church of the Ognissanti, Florence.

18, 19, 20 *Primavera*; and two details. c. 1478. Panel. $70 \times 123\frac{5}{8}$ in. (203 × 314 cm.). Uffizi, Florence.

21 *Scenes from the Life of Moses.* 1481–82. Fresco. 11 ft. 5 in × 18 ft. $3\frac{3}{4}$ in. (348 × 558 cm.). Sistine Chapel, Vatican.

22 *Purification of the Leper and Temptation of Christ.* 1481–82. Fresco. 11 ft. 4 in. × 5 ft. 1 in. (345.5 × 555 cm.). Sistine Chapel, Vatican.

23, 24 *Destruction of Korah and his associates*; and detail. 1481–82. Fresco. 11 ft. 5 in. × 18 ft. $8\frac{1}{2}$ in. (348.5 × 570 cm.). Sistine Chapel, Vatican.

25 *Portrait of Dante.* c. 1480–85. Canvas. $21\frac{1}{4} \times 18\frac{1}{2}$ in. (54.5 × 47.5 cm.). Collection Dr Martin Bodmer, Cologny/Geneva.

26 *Pallas and the Centaur.* c. 1482. Canvas. $81\frac{1}{2} \times 58\frac{1}{4}$ in. (207 × 148 cm.). Uffizi, Florence.

27 *Madonna of the Magnificat.* c. 1482. Panel. Diameter $46\frac{1}{2}$ in. (118 cm.). Uffizi, Florence.

28 *Portrait of a Young Man.* c. 1482. Panel. $14\frac{3}{4} \times 11$ in. (37.5 × 28 cm.). National Gallery, London.

29 *Young Man Presented to the Seven Liberal Arts.* c. 1483. Fresco from the Villa Lemmi, Florence. $89\frac{3}{8} \times 81\frac{7}{8}$ in. (227 × 269 cm.). Louvre, Paris.

30 *Young Woman with Venus and the Graces.* c. 1483. Fresco from the Villa Lemmi, Florence. $84 \times 111\frac{3}{4}$ in. (212 × 284 cm.). Louvre, Paris.

31 *Madonna with St John the Baptist and St John the Evangelist.* 1485. Panel. $73 \times 70\frac{7}{8}$ in. (185 × 180 cm.). Staatliche Museen, Gemäldegalerie, Berlin-Dahlem.

32 *Birth of Venus.* c. 1485–86. Canvas. $68 \times 109\frac{1}{2}$ in. (172.5 × 278.5 cm.). Uffizi, Florence.

33, 34 *Venus and Mars*; and detail. c. 1485–86. Panel. $27\frac{1}{4} \times 68\frac{1}{4}$ in. (69 × 173 cm.). National Gallery, London.

35 *Madonna of the Pomegranate.* c. 1487. Panel. Diameter $56\frac{1}{2}$ in. (143.5 cm.). Uffizi, Florence.

36 *Altarpiece of San Barnaba.* c. 1488. Panel. 8 ft. $9\frac{1}{2}$ in. × 9 ft. 2 in. (268 × 280 cm.). Uffizi, Florence.

37 *St Augustine's Vision of the Child on the Shore.* c. 1488. Panel. $7\frac{7}{8} \times 15$ in. (20 × 38 cm.). Uffizi, Florence.

38, 39 *Annunciation*; and detail. c. 1489–90. Panel. $59 \times 61\frac{1}{2}$ in. (150 × 156 cm.). Uffizi, Florence.

40 *St Augustine in his Study.* c. 1490. Panel. $16\frac{1}{8} \times 10\frac{5}{8}$ in. (41 × 27 cm.). Uffizi, Florence.

41 *Calumny.* c. 1494–95. Panel. $24\frac{1}{2} \times 36$ in. (62 × 91 cm.). Uffizi, Florence.

42 *Story of Virginia.* c. 1499. Panel. $33\frac{7}{8} \times 65$ in. (86 × 165 cm.). Galleria dell' Accademia Carrara, Bergamo.

43 *The Tragedy of Lucretia.* c. 1499. Panel. $31\frac{1}{2} \times 70$ in. (80 × 178 cm.). Isabella Stewart Gardner Museum, Boston.

44 *Miracles of St Zenobius.* c. 1500–05. Panel. $25\frac{1}{2} \times 54\frac{3}{4}$ in. (65 × 139.5 cm.). National Gallery, London.

45 *Pietà.* c. 1490–1500. Panel. $42\frac{1}{8} \times 28$ in. (107 × 71 cm.). Poldi-Pezzoli Collection, Milan.

46 *Pietà.* c. 1490–1500. Panel. $43\frac{1}{4} \times 81\frac{1}{2}$ in. (110 × 207 cm.). Alte Pinakothek, Munich.

47 *Last Communion of St Jerome.* c. 1496–1500. Panel. $13 \times 13\frac{3}{4}$ in. (33 × 35 cm.). Bequest of Benjamin Altman, 1913. Metropolitan Museum of Art, New York.

48 *Mystic Crucifixion.* c. 1501. Canvas. $28\frac{3}{4} \times 20$ in. (73 × 51 cm.). Courtesy Fogg Art Museum, Cambridge, Mass. Harvard University: Gift of the Friends of the Fogg Art Museum.

49 *Mystic Nativity.* 1501. Canvas. $42\frac{1}{2} \times 29\frac{1}{2}$ in. (108.5 × 75 cm.). National Gallery, London.

50 *Agony in the Garden.* c. 1504. Panel. $20\frac{7}{8} \times 13\frac{3}{4}$ in. (53 × 35 cm.). Royal Chapel, Granada.

Acknowledgements
The following photographs were supplied by:
Accademia Carrara, Bergamo, 42;
Joachim Blauel, Munich, 46;
Fogg Art Museum, Cambridge, Massachusetts, 48;
Isabella Stewart Gardner Museum, Boston, Massachusetts, 7, 43;
Hamlyn Group Picture Library, 1, 4, 6, 9, 11, 14, 15, 21, 22, 23, 24, 28, 35, 36, 37, 40;
Hans Hinz, Basle, 25, 50;

Metropolitan Museum of Art, New York, 47;
National Gallery, London, 8, 33, 34, 44, 49;
National Gallery of Art, Washington, 10;
Photographie Giraudon, Paris, 29;
Scala, Antella, 2, 3, 5, 12, 16, 17, 18, 19, 20, 26, 27, 32, 38, 39, 41, 45;
Service de Documentation, Versailles, 30;
Staatliche Museen, Gemäldegalerie, Berlin–Dahlem, 13, 31.

1

2

4

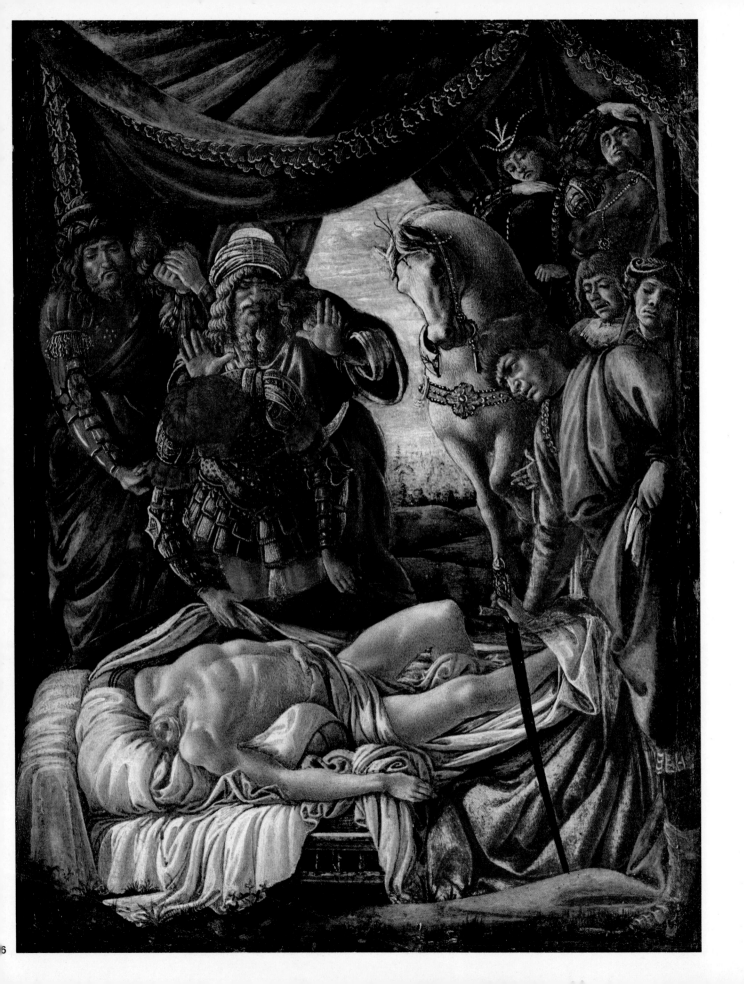

8

9

14

15

16

17

21

29

30

3

3

42

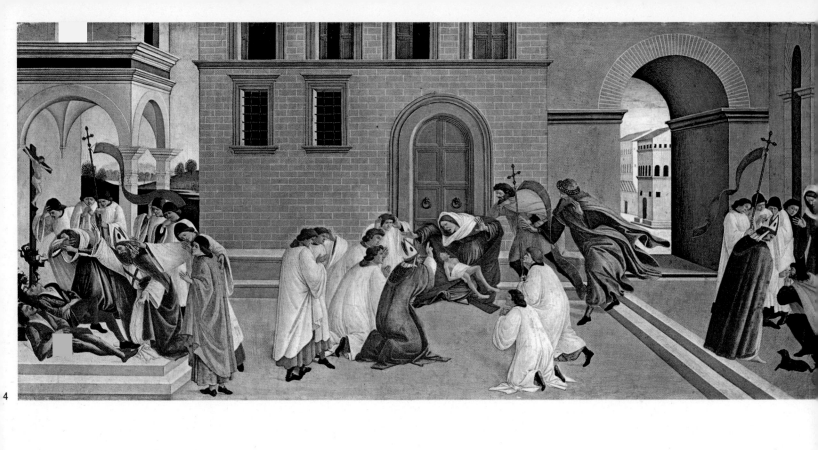

4

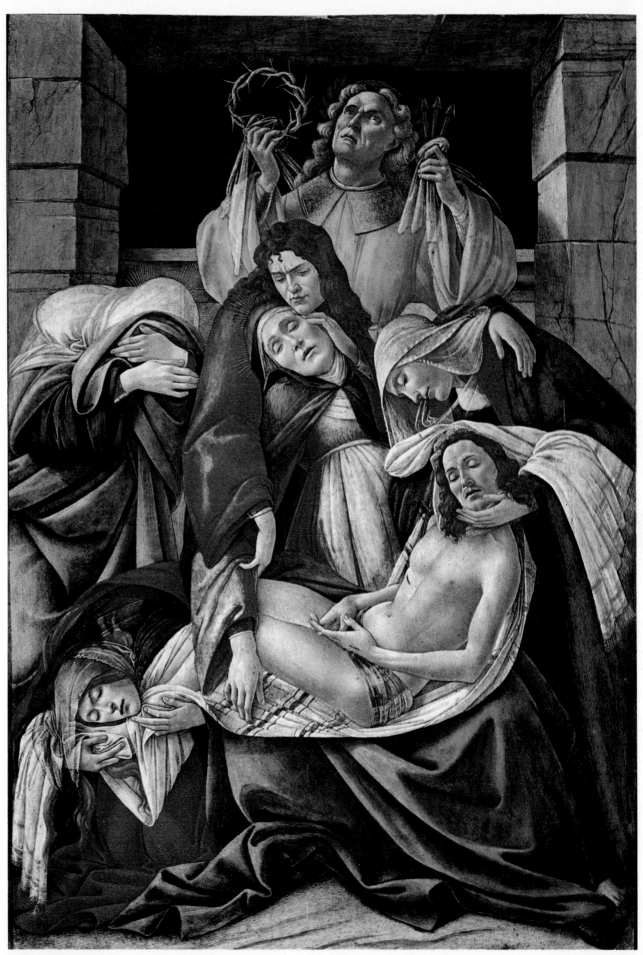

6

Titian

Most of us think of artists as exceptional men who must pay some kind of penalty for their gifts. They suffer in mind or body, blunder in the ordinary affairs of life, or die poor and unrecognised. One or another of these descriptions fits a host of artists from Leonardo da Vinci to Vincent van Gogh.

But none of them fits Titian. His was one of the greatest of all success stories. He was rich and famous in his own lifetime, and has never been out of fashion in the four centuries since his death. He was healthy and prolific, turning out a steady stream of pictures into advanced old age. And although he was a considerable innovator, he never lacked buyers for his works or respectful friends among the great men of his time.

The main setting for this wonderful career was the city of Venice, then one of the great commercial powers of Europe. Centuries of virtual control of trade with the East had made the city enormously wealthy. Her power extended inland to Italian cities such as Padua and Verona, while there were coastal strips and islands under Venetian rule all the way along the Dalmatian coast to Greece; Cyprus, Crete and the Ionian islands, though increasingly threatened by the might of Turkey, were all Venetian possessions in Titian's day. A city of sumptuous golden buildings, canals and lagoons, Venice is famed for effects of light and colour which have certainly helped to create the great tradition of Venetian painting.

Titian, however, was a provincial. Tiziano Vecellio (to give him his Italian name) was born at Cadore, a mountain village in the Dolomites, probably around 1487–90. According to Vasari he arrived in Venice when he was about ten years old, staying with an uncle who was a respected Venetian citizen. When his talent as a painter became apparent, Titian was apprenticed to the leading painters in Venice, Gentile and Giovanni Bellini.

But the biggest influence on Titian's early career was a painter only a few years older than he was: Giorgio da Castelfranco, called Giorgione, who introduced a style with softened tones and outlines that revolutionised Venetian art. Though never Giorgione's pupil, Titian took over his technique along with his lyrical mood and unprecedented emphasis on landscape. This 'Giorgionesque' approach is apparent in *The Three Ages of Man* (plate 3); its golden landscape heightens the poetic feeling for the brevity of childhood and youth, while softening the grim presence of the feeble old man bent over his skulls. *Sacred and Profane Love* (plates 6–8) is an even greater masterpriece in which the landscape forms an integral part of the grave, mysteriously evocative mood.

At this period of his life Titian was so much the disciple of Giorgione that experts have found it hard to decide which of them painted a given picture. In the case of a number of works, such as *Noli Me Tangere* (plate 5), it has been suggested that Titian finished what Giorgione had begun. This seems quite likely in view of Giorgione's early death, probably caused by the plague, in 1510.

In the next few years Titian moved towards his first peak of eminence. In 1511 he was given his first commission outside Venice itself, painting a series of frescos including *St Anthony Healing the Youth's Leg* (plate 2) for the Scuola del

Santo in Padua. Though landscape always remained an important element in his work, he was beginning to paint in a less dreamlike style and to give greater prominence to the human actors in his pictures. *The Gypsy Madonna* (plate 9) and *The Madonna with the Cherries* (plate 10) must belong to this period.

Giorgione's death was shortly followed by the departure for Rome of his gifted pupil Sebastiono del Piombo. And so when Giovanni Bellini died in 1516 Titian had no serious rival for the official post of chief painter to the Venetian Republic. He was already a success.

He celebrated by painting a gigantic altarpiece for the Venetian church of the Frari. The revolutionary nature of *The Assumption of the Virgin* (plates 11, 12) can be grasped by simply comparing it with the plates in this book immediately preceding it. Without warning we are plunged into a scene of frenzied movement and almost hysterical emotion, bathed in a rich, fierce light. Nothing like the extraordinary energy of this picture had been seen before in Venice, and its style was not to gain wide currency until the next century. *The Madonna of the Pesaro Family* in the same church (plate 13) contains a different sort of innovation. All Titian did was to place the Madonna to one side of the picture instead of following convention and putting her in the centre. This kind of new development in composition is hard to appreciate after the event (especially since its use and re-use by later artists deprives it of impact), yet a 'simple' change such as this—from symmetry to assymmetry—opens up a multitude of new possibilities in design. Incidentally the kneeling man on the left is Jacopo Pesaro, Bishop of

Paphos, who is also shown in plate 1 being presented to St Peter by Pope Alexander VI.

In the 1520s Titian was becoming well known outside the Venetian territories. For Alfonso of Ferrara he painted a light-filled, joyously crowded series of bacchanals, mythological paintings in which wine, or Bacchus the god of wine, is the subject. *The Bacchanal of the Andrians* (plate 15) is suggested by the mythical river of wine on the island of Andros. *Bacchus and Ariadne* (plate 16), one of Titian's most famous pictures, is based on the myth of Ariadne, who helped Theseus to slay the Minotaur but was deserted by him on the island of Naxos, where Bacchus found her and made her his wife. In Titian's painting Bacchus is not making a good first impression: he and his noisy, tipsy rout have evidently alarmed her. The eye is irresistably drawn to the strange wild figure of Bacchus himself, but it is well worth pulling back and examining the many interesting details and the splendid landscape—a feature easily overlooked and yet decisive in creating the atmosphere of the painting.

The Entombment (plate 17), painted for the duke of Mantua, is perhaps Titian's most shattering picture. We can define some of the devices used—the play of light and dark, the way in which the attention is focused within an area bounded by the blue of the Virgin's mantle and the opulent red silk of the unknown helper's coat; but the total effect defies analysis. Here, as elsewhere, Titian captures the weight and 'presence' of the human body. The dead man's heavy, creased flesh, Joseph of Aramathea's beautiful forearm and the helper's meaty legs give the scene its stamp of physical actuality. Yet the overall impression is not of human tragedy, however frightful, but of a cataclysmic event, of the slaying of a Man-God.

There could hardly be a greater contrast to the *Entombment* than the *Venus of Urbino* (plate 18), painted for the duke of Urbino some years later. This is Titian as his most worldly, taking obvious sensual delight in the warm living flesh and the elaborately crumpled sheets. The pose is almost identical with that of a Venus by Giorgione which is said to have been one of the paintings completed by Titian. But Giorgione's Venus is innocently asleep in an enchanted landscape: Titian's, languorous in the boudoir and with her eyes fixed on the spectator, has been expelled from Eden long ago.

For all his skill as a mythological and religious painter, what recommended Titian above all to patrons was his skill as a portraitist. In his time the portrait was coming into its own. Instead of a plain head and shoulders (like a coloured passport photograph) the sitter was shown half or full length, and perhaps, dramatically, from an angle, as in plates 19–21 and the famous Paul III (plate 27). Here Titian was without question supreme in his own time, and with few rivals in the whole history of painting. His gift for creating a sense of physical presence was brought into full play. The young man in plate 19 has an exceptional quality of suppressed energy, but the other portraits are also notable for the in-dwelling personal force of the sitters. They are not nonentities hiding behind elaborate costumes: Philip II is man enough to own—and not be owned by—his wonderful armour; and even the shrunken, rat-like pope (plate 28), apparently cowering away during a furious row

with his grandsons, has a resistant personal core that Titian cleverly brings out by using light to mute the rich colouring of the pope's cap and mantle.

Apart from its other merits, this kind of treatment was flattering in the extreme. It made Titian the busiest painter of his time and persuaded dukes and princes to put up with his slowness and his constant demands for money. (Writers have held this up as an unflattering aspect of Titian's character. It seems natural enough in view of the 16th-century ruler's habit of going bankrupt every few years and ruining his creditors.) He was also fortunate in his friendship with Pietro Aretino, who knew—and intimidated—most of Europe's princes. Aretino was the most inventively scurrilous writer of his time, with a capacity for invective that made every public man eager to be his generous friend rather than his butt. Titian's portrait of Aretino (plate 23) shows a man of bull-like force whom it would be dangerous to cross. He introduced Titian to many of his patrons and may well have been responsible for the artist's decisive encounter with the Emperor Charles V.

Charles was the most powerful man in Europe. Through the advantageous marriages contracted by his family, the Habsburgs, he had inherited the Holy Roman Empire (a rather larger area than modern Germany), Spain, the Netherlands, and most of Central and South America. An empire this size was as much a burden as a source of strength, and Charles spent most of his long reign in a successful but exhausting holding operation against the French, the Turks, and the Protestant heretics in his German dominions. Something of this appears in Titian's portraits of the emperor—in the famous equestrian portrait which remained a model for other painters for centuries, and in the portrait of Charles seated, strong of will but borne down by the cares of ruling half the world.

Charles delighted in Titian's art and rewarded him lavishly. He ennobled the painter, treated him as a friend, and is even said to have stooped to pick up one of Titian's brushes. No artist had ever been treated like this before—not even Leonardo or Michelangelo. If in the next century artists blossomed into courtiers and diplomats, it was largely thanks to Titian.

The patronage of Charles V set the seal on Titian's fame. Vasari tells us that it is a waste of time to list Titian's portraits: he has painted almost everybody of any eminence in Europe. (But no Englishmen, unless the unknown young man in plate 22 is really the 'young Englishman' or 'duke of Norfolk' of tradition. To Vasari, England was doubtless a remote, half-civilised spot on the edge of Christendom.) Titian painted Pope Paul when the pontiff visited Ferrara in 1543, and two years later visited the Eternal City for the first time. There he painted Paul and his quarrelsome 'nephews', a tactful euphemism applied to the children and (as here) grand-children of Renaissance popes. He was shown around by the ubiquitous Vasari, who also took Michelangelo to see him. The two visitors praised his paintings to his face, but started to criticize them after they had left together. Michelangelo praised Titian's natural gifts but remarked that it was a pity the Venetians neglected the study of drawing. What in fact put Michelangelo off was the revolutionary new style that Titian was developing, a subject to

which we shall have to return.

In 1556, worn out by forty years of struggle, Charles V retired to the monastery of Yuste in Spain. With him he took the altarpiece *La Gloria* (plates 30–32), in which he is the most prominent of the worshippers (on the far left in the smaller detail, plate 31). Not far behind him is his son and successor as king of Spain, Philip II— unmistakeably the same man as the splendid armoured prince (plate 29).

Philip had been Titian's patron since 1548, when the two men met at Milan. Now he became the painter's chief customer, commissioning so many pictures (and proving so willing to accept any others that Titian took it into his head to send him) that Titian rarely bothered to work for anyone else. Philip's specific demand was for a series of mythological paintings, partly at least because myth provided a respectable cover for erotic subjects. In *Danäe* (plate 38) the amorous god Zeus is having his way by changing himself into a shower of gold; in *The Rape of Europa* (plate 44) he has varied his technique, turning himself into a bull. *Venus and Adonis* (plate 39) shows the goddess making strenuous efforts to divert Adonis from his fatal hunting trip (he was killed by a wild boar). In *Diana and Actaeon* (plates 40, 41) the women do not seem too displeased at the accident which has led a young man to discover them bathing. However, the myth has it that the young man was Actaeon, who was turned into a stag and torn to pieces because he saw Diana naked. Diana was goddess of the hunt and vowed to chastity; hence the scandal of plates 42 and 43, in which the attendant nymph Calisto is found to be with child. Finally, *The Rape of Lucretia* (plate 45) concerns the Roman matron raped by King Tarquin of Rome. Her suicide led to a revolt and the expulsion of kings from Rome – an ostensibly republican subject that reinforces our impression that Philip's mind was not on mythology or history when he looked at these pictures.

Titian's late style, whether in mythological or religious paintings, became increasingly unorthodox; Vasari even thought it a shame that Titian should have lowered his reputation with such senile productions. The skilful orthodox painter created firmly outlined figures and gave his pictures a smooth finish, with no visible brushstrokes or blobs of paint. But Titian was moving in the opposite direction. He was using areas of colour to define his forms and blobs of paint to convey something of the brilliant, irregular appearance of things seen under strong light. One of Titian's assistants, Palma Giovanne, has described the way in which the old man would tackle one painting or another according to his mood, often working the paint on to the picture surface with his fingers.

The 'impressionistic' result is more apparent in some of his later works than in others. For example *Nymph and Shepherd* (plate 47) at once strikes us as an 'unfinished' work in Titian's 'painterly' style. So does the landscape in *The Rape of Europa* (plate 44), which might be a different hand from that of the bacchanals. Even more instructive is a comparison between two versions of *Christ Crowned with Thorns*. The earlier (plate 37) is full of pathos and violence, reinforced by lighting. Like the late *Entombment* (plate 48) it marks a kind of return to the energetic dramatic manner of *The Assumption* (plate 11). In the later *Christ Crowned with Thorns* (plate 50) the mood is quieter and more resigned, but it is Titian's use of paint that is really astonishing. Even in reproduction we can see the dabs of paint and brushstrokes that create the flares, the highlights on Jesus's chest and shoulders, the rich clothing of the tormentor with his back to us, and many other details.

Titian worked on, apparently indestructible, until he was carried off by the plague in 1576. Though Venice produced great masters before and after him, he is by common consent the greatest of all the city's artists.

THE PLATES

1 *Pope Alexander VI presents Jacopo Pesaro to St Peter.* Canvas. 57¼ × 72½ in. (145 × 183 cm.). Musée des Beaux-Arts, Antwerp.

2 *St Anthony Healing the Youth's Leg.* 1511. Fresco. Scuola del Santo, Padua.

3 *Three Ages of Man.* ?c. 1511. Canvas. 42 × 72 in. (106 × 182 cm.). Duke of Sutherland Collection, on loan to National Gallery of Scotland, Edinburgh.

4 *Baptism of Christ.* Canvas. 45½ × 35 in. (115 × 89 cm.). Pinacoteca Capitolina, Rome.

5 *Noli me Tangere.* ?1512. Canvas. 42¾ × 35¾ in. (109 × 91 cm.). National Gallery, London.

6, 7, 8 *Sacred and Profane Love.* Canvas. 46¾ × 111 in. (118 × 279 cm.). Villa Borghese, Rome.

9 *Gypsy Madonna.* Canvas. 25½ × 32½ in. (68.9 × 83.5 cm.). Kunsthistorisches Museum, Vienna.

10 *Madonna with the Cherries.* Canvas. 31½ × 39⅜ in. (81 × 99.5 cm.). Kunsthistorisches Museum, Vienna.

11, 12 *Assumption of the Virgin. c.* 1518. Canvas. 272 × 142 in. (691 × 360 cm.). Church of the Frari, Venice.

13 *Madonna of the Pesaro Family.* 1519–26. Canvas. 191 × 106½ in. (485 × 270 cm.). Church of the Frari, Venice.

14 *St Sebastian.* 1522. Canvas. 66 × 28 in. (167 × 63 cm.). Church of SS Nazaro and Celso, Brescia.

15 *Bacchanal of the Andrians. c.* 1522. Canvas. 69 × 76 in. 175 × 193 cm.). Prado, Madrid.

16 *Bacchus and Ariadne. c.* 1522. Canvas. 69 × 76 in. (175 × 190 cm.). National Gallery, London.

17 *Entombment of Christ. c.* 1522. Canvas. 58¾ × 84¾ in. (148 × 218 cm.). Louvre, Paris.

18 *Venus of Urbino.* 1538. Canvas. 64¾ × 76½ in. (165 × 195 cm.). Uffizi, Florence.

19 *Portrait of a Venetian Gentleman.* Canvas. 29¾ × 24⅞ in. (76 × 63 cm.). National Gallery of Art (Samuel H. Kress Collection), Washington DC.

20 *Portrait of a Man.* Canvas. 32 × 26 in. (81.2 × 66.3 cm.). National Gallery, London.

21 *Portrait of a Young Man. c.* 1520. Canvas. 39½ × 33 in. (100 × 84 cm.). Earl of Halifax, Garrowby Hall, York.

22 *Portrait of a Young Man.* Canvas. 44 × 37 in. (111 × 93 cm.). Palazzo Pitti, Florence.

23 *Portrait of Pietro Aretino.* Canvas. 39¼ × 32 in. (99 × 82 cm.). Frick Collection, New York.

24 *The Vendramin Family.* Canvas. 81 × 118½ in. (206 × 301 cm.). National Gallery, London.

25, 26 *Presentation of the Virgin. c.* 1535. Canvas. 136 × 295 in. (345 × 775 cm.). Accademia, Venice.

27 *Portrait of Pope Paul III.* 1543. 42 × 32 in. (106 × 82 cm.). Capodimonte Gallery, Naples.

28 *Portrait of Pope Paul III and his 'Nephews',* 1545/6. 83 × 68¾ in. (210 × 174 cm.). Capodimonte Gallery, Naples.

29 *Portrait of Philip II of Spain in Armour.* Canvas. 76 × 44 in. (193 × 111 cm.). Prado, Madrid.

30, 31, 32 *La Gloria.* Canvas. 136¾ × 95 in. (346 × 240 cm.). Prado, Madrid.

33, 34, 35 *Ecce Homo.* 1554. Canvas. 95 × 142 in. (240 × 360 cm.). Kunsthistorisches Museum, Vienna.

36 *St Jerome.* Canvas. 93 × 49¼ in. (235 × 125 cm.). Brera, Milan.

37 *Christ Crowned with Thorns.* Canvas. 119 × 70¾ in. (303 × 180 cm.). Louvre, Paris.

38 *Danäe.* 1554. Canvas. 50½ × 70 in. (128 × 178 cm). Prado, Madrid.

39 *Venus and Adonis.* 1554. Canvas. 73½ × 81¾ in. (186 × 207 cm.). Prado, Madrid.

40, 41 *Diana and Actaeon.* Canvas. 75 × 81¾ in. (190.5 × 207 cm.). Duke of Sutherland Collection, on loan to National Gallery of Scotland, Edinburgh.

42, 43 *Diana and Callisto.* Canvas. 75 × 81¾ in. (190.5 × 207 cm.). Duke of Sutherland Collection, on loan to National Gallery of Scotland, Edinburgh.

44 *The Rape of Europa.* 1558. Canvas. 64¼ × 80¾ in. (176 × 204 cm.). Isabella Stewart Gardner Museum, Boston.

45 *The Rape of Lucretia.* 1571. Canvas. 74⅛ × 57½ in. (187.5 × 145 cm.). Fitzwilliam Museum, Cambridge.

46 *Education of Cupid.* Canvas. 46¾ × 73 in. (118 × 185 cm.). Villa Borghese, Rome.

47 *Nymph and Shepherd*. Canvas. 56 × 74 in. (142 × 187 cm.). Kunsthistorisches Museum, Vienna.

48 *Entombment of Christ*. Canvas. 54 × 69 in. (137 × 175 cm.). Prado, Madrid.

49 *Annunciation*. Canvas. 162 × 105 in. (410 × 240 cm.). Church of San Salvatore, Venice.

50 *Christ Crowned with Thorns*. Canvas. 110½ × 72 in. (280 × 182 cm.). Alte Pinakothek, Munich.

51 *Portrait of Jacopo Strada*. 1567/8. Canvas. 52 × 37⅓ in. (125 × 95 cm.). Kunsthistorisches Museum, Vienna.

52 *Pietà*. Canvas. 138¾ × 153¾ in. (351 × 389 cm.). Accademia, Venice.

Acknowledgements
The following photographs were supplied by:
Alinari, Florence, 25, 30;
Joachim Blauel, Munich, 50;
Brera, Milan, 36;
Harold Bridge, New York, 21;
Fitzwilliam Museum, Cambridge, 45;
Frick Collection, New York, 23;
Isabella Stewart Gardner Museum, Boston, Massachusetts, 44;
Hamlyn Group Picture Library, 3, 9, 10, 14, 15, 40, 41, 42, 43;
Koninklijk Museum voor Schone Kunsten, Antwerp, 1.
Kunsthistorisches Museum, Vienna, 33, 34, 35, 47, 51;
Mansell Collection, London 11;
National Gallery, London, 5, 16, 20, 24;
National Gallery of Art, Washington 19;
Mauro Pucciarelli, Rome, 4, 46;
Réunion des Musées Nationaux, Paris, 17, 37;
Scala, Antella, 2, 6, 7, 8, 12, 13, 18, 22, 26, 27, 28, 29, 31, 32, 38, 39, 48, 49, 52.

1

3

9

6

7

14

16

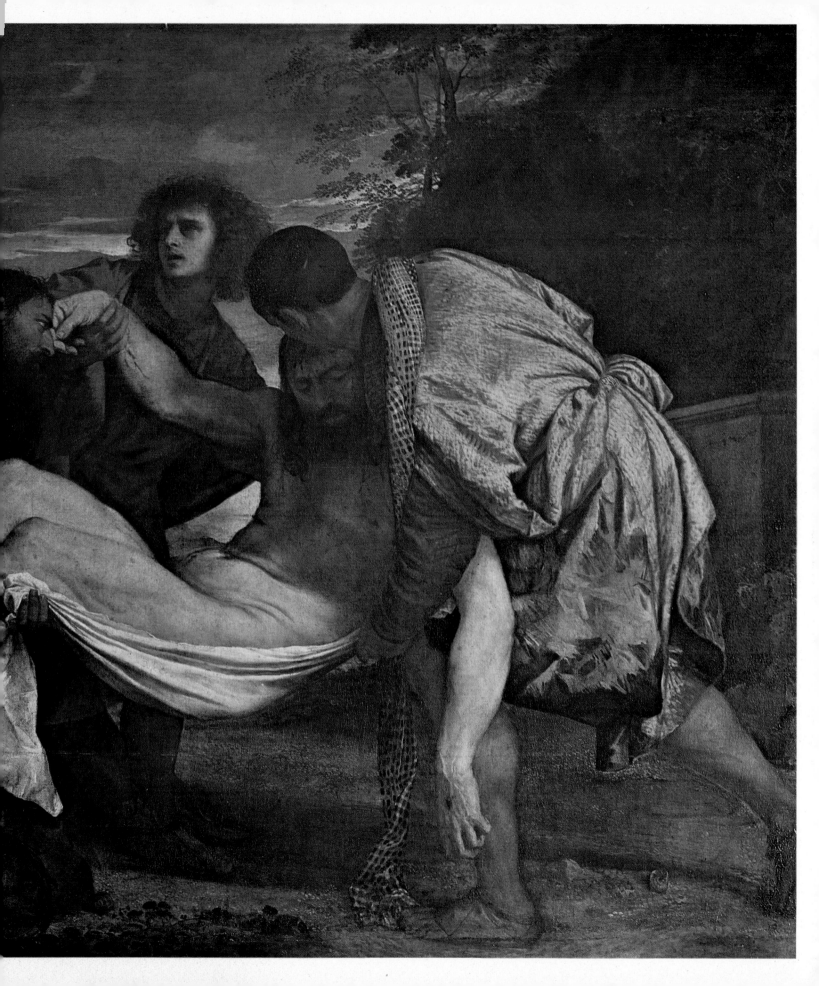

18

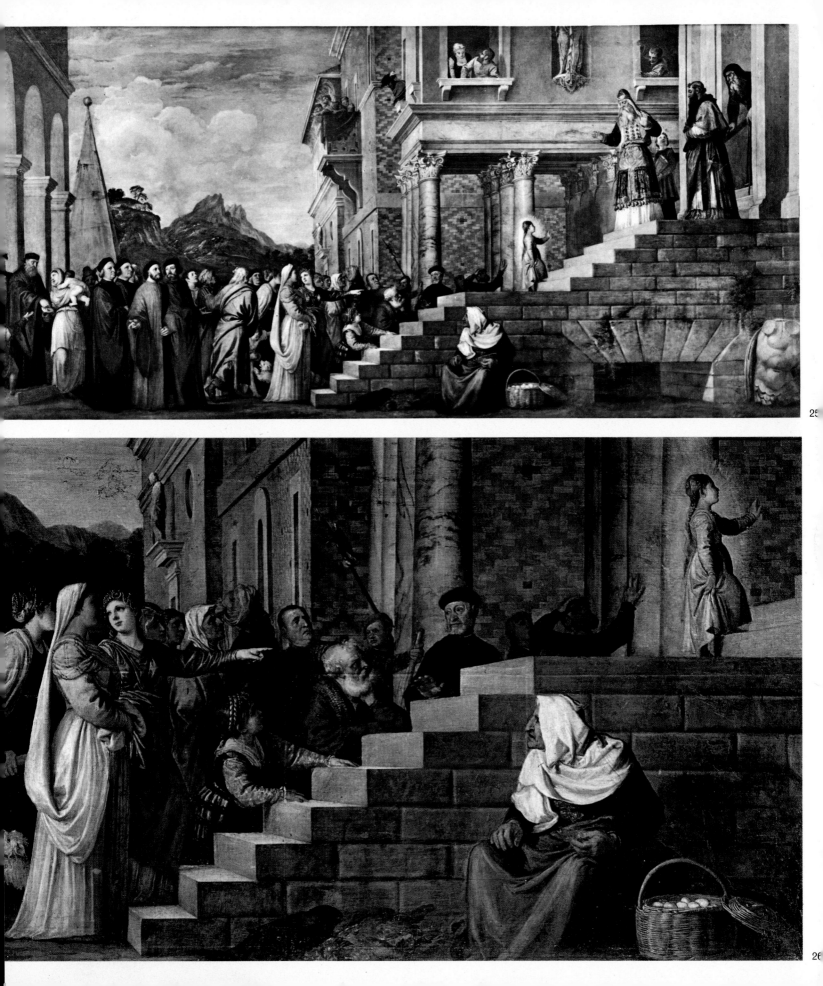

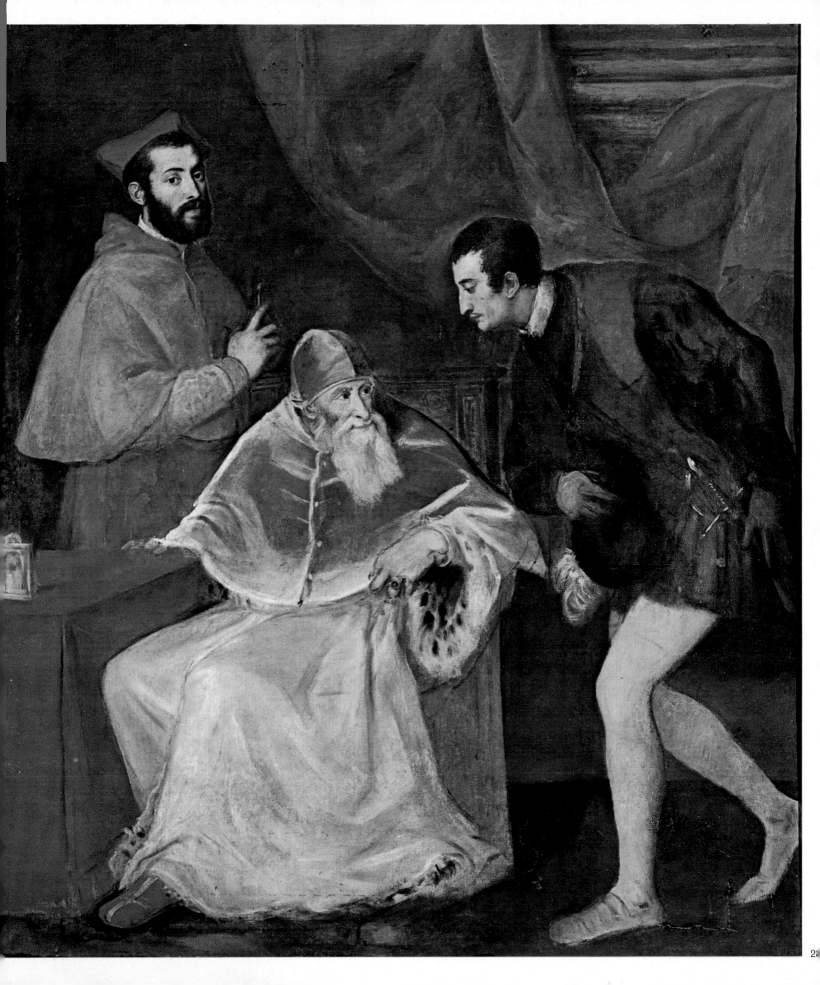

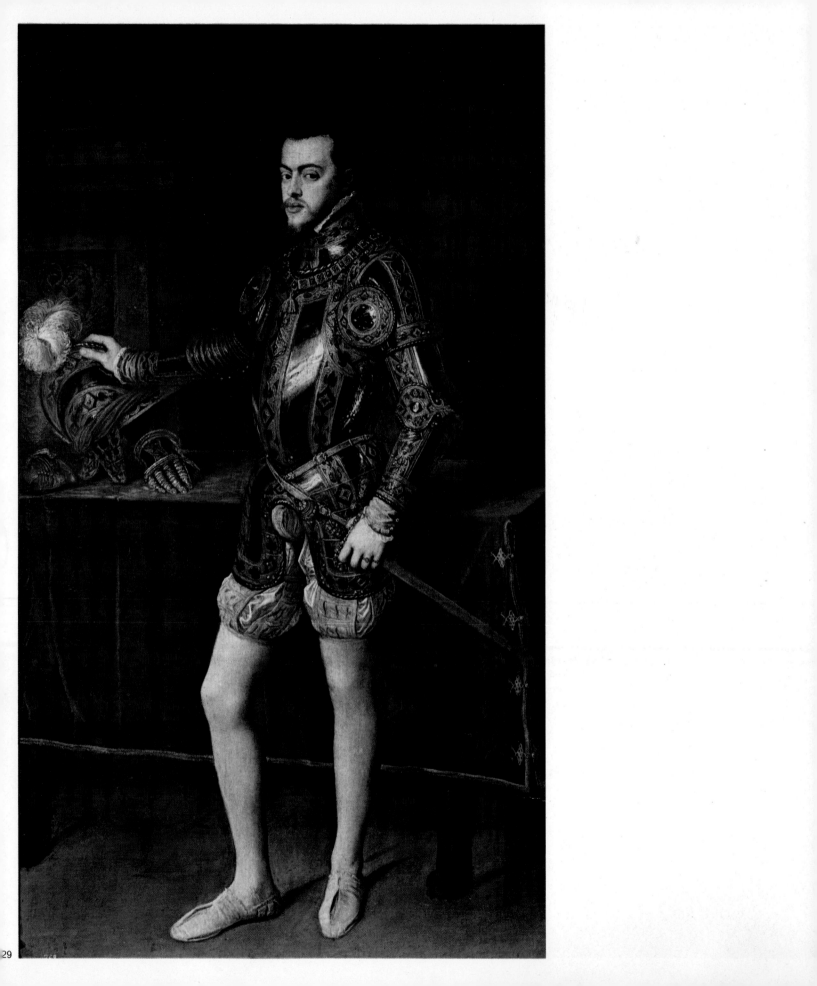

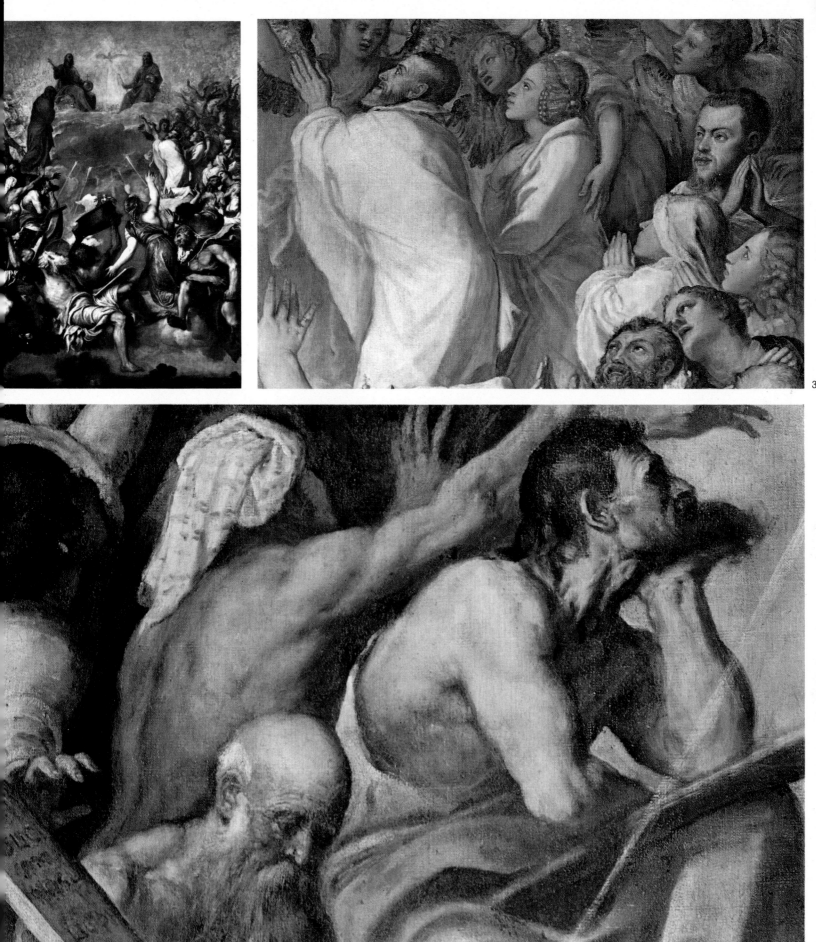

3

4

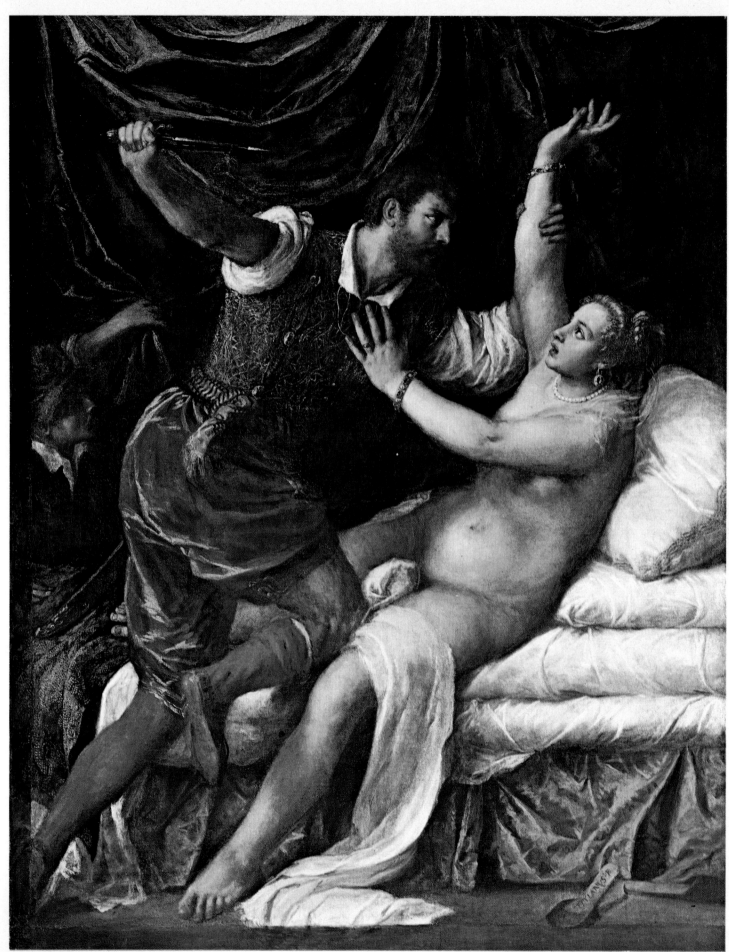

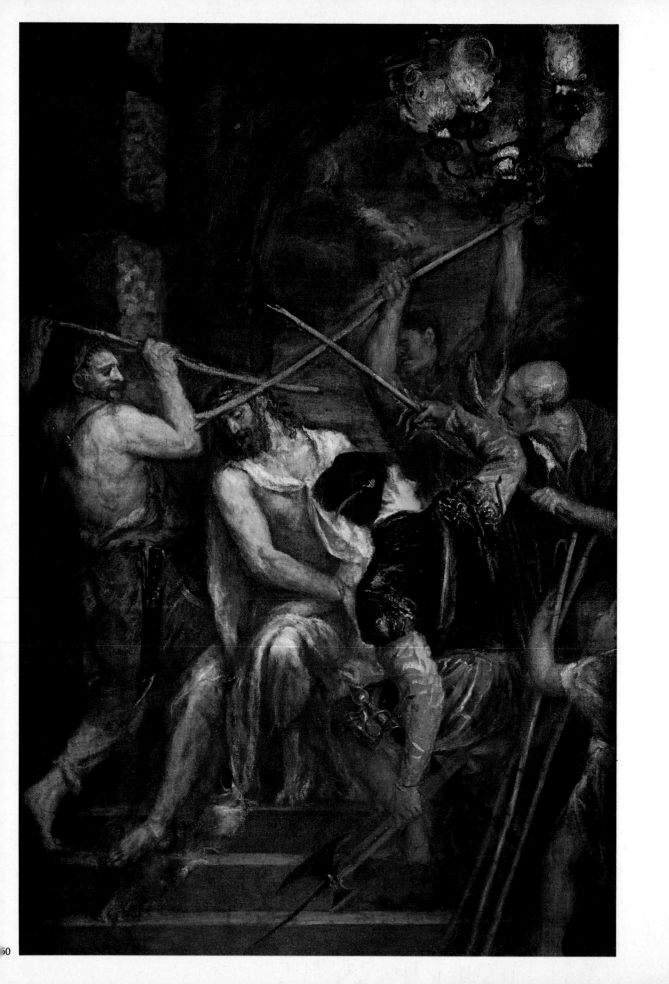

TITIANVS F

IACOBVS DE S[...]
[...]VIS ROMANV[...]
[...]TIONARIVS E[...]
[...] AN [...]

51

QVOD TITIANVS INCHOATV M. RELIQVIT
PALMA REVERENTER ABSOLVIT
DEOQ. DICAVIT OPVS

52

Watteau

After the paintings of Botticelli and Titian, Watteau's works come as a shock. Suddenly there is almost no place for the religious intensities and elaborate mythologies that had dominated painting for hundreds of years. Watteau's art is entirely worldly and, as it seems, unserious. In his warm, romantic landscapes, elegant fancy-dress figures engage in lovemaking, talk and music. This is an aristocratic never-never land from which war, politics and poverty—and even disease and death—have been banished.

The type of picture in which all this happens, called a *fête galante*, was virtually Watteau's invention. But the worldly, frivolous mood was that of the time in which he lived. When he arrived in Paris, the long reign of Louis XIV was drawing to a close. In his days of glory Louis had favoured a heavy 'classical' style, which in painting meant a pompous mixture of mythology and celebration of the king's victories. But as the glory faded with each French disaster in the War of the Spanish Succession, everybody—even the king himself—felt the need for a lighter, less pretentious style. The need was soon answered in Rococo, a gay, curvacious, soft-coloured style that affected all the arts of interior design. With the end of the war and the death of the old king in 1715, Frenchmen followed the lead of their new ruler, the Regent Philippe d'Orléans, and gave themselves up wholeheartedly to the pursuit of pleasure.

Watteau's paintings certainly reflect the same kind of mood—one which, with variations, was dominant in French art down to the 1760s. But he is a great artist just because he goes beyond the mood of the moment. Even at first glance his scenes of light-hearted dalliance are tinged with sadness. Its precise meaning escapes us, though it seems to have something to do with nostalgia for lost illusions or a bitter-sweet sense that time and love are passing away. Watteau gives us enchanted moments, but moments whose transience is keenly felt.

Descriptions of Watteau's character are interesting but not very helpful: his friends clearly found him an enigma. Like many artists he was both timid and fierce. He was often cold and sarcastic, but he had a gift for making valuable contacts and loyal friends who would commission paintings and put him up for long periods. (He needed such friends. He was compulsively restless, and constantly moved from one lodging to another.) His friends put up with his idiosyncrasies, believing (rightly or wrongly) that they stemmed from his bad health and feelings of inferiority because of his lack of education. Finally, he was, as we should expect such a difficult man to be, a perfectionist, never satisfied with what he had done.

The facts of Watteau's life are equally poor in clues. This painter of aristocratic sophistication was a rank provincial. He was born in 1684 at Valenciennes, a little town in northern France that had been annexed from Flanders only six years before Watteau's birth; in fact Watteau's contemporaries tended to look on him as a Flemish rather than a French painter. His father, a reasonably prosperous builder, apprenticed him to a painter in the town called Gérin, who probably died soon afterwards. At any rate Watteau found another master and about 1702 accompanied him to Paris. They were employed as scene painters at the Paris Opera, but when the job ended the master went back to

Valenciennes. His pupil stayed on in Paris and was soon struggling. Eventually he was taken on by a picture factory on the Notre Dame bridge. There, for three livres a week, Watteau formed part of a human conveyor belt; he painted the figures in a scene, another artist painted skies, another draperies, and so on down the line. The situation must have seemed the more galling in that much of the work consisted of copying established Flemish and Dutch masters.

Watteau's luck must have turned fairly quickly, for by about 1703 he had started a new apprenticeship with a bona fide artist. This was Claude Gillot, whose paintings of scenes from the theatre were a major influence on Watteau, at least as far as subject matter is concerned. Watteau stayed with Gillot for four or five years. Then he left to become the assistant of Claude Audran III, who was a member of a prolific dynasty of decorative artists. Watteau helped Audran decorate châteaux and town houses, and was given sufficient responsibility for us to be able to pick out some of his contributions.

The *Singerie* (plate 1) is a sketch for a wall painting to be done at the château of Marly. The *singerie*, a humorous type of design in which monkeys were shown behaving like people, was a popular decorative device of the time. The flowing leafy scrolls are the hallmark of the Rococo style and also occur in *The Cajoler* and *The Faun* (plates 2, 3), which are part of a series of eight panels originally painted for the Hôtel de Nointel in Paris. Watteau's association with Audran also enabled him to study some paintings by the great Flemish master Peter Paul Rubens; these were kept in the Luxembourg Palace, of which Audran was keeper. Watteau learned much

from Rubens's achievements as a colourist, but despite his drawing of a couple after Rubens's *La Kermesse* (plate 4), that master's sensual swirling energy remained foreign to Watteau's temperament.

Watteau's career as an independent artist seems to have started about 1709. In traditional style he entered a Biblical painting, *David and Nabal* (now lost), for the Rome prize, but could only come second. He also painted some pictures of soldiers in camp or on the march (plates 6, 7) which may or may not have occasioned a short visit to Valenciennes, then a garrison town.

Suddenly, after his long and obscure apprenticeship, we hear of Watteau as a successful painter. He is taken up by the dealer Sirois, with whom he lodges for some time, and is besieged by would-be clients. In 1712 he achieves the accolade of conventional success, becoming an associate of the French Academy. To become a full member he needs only to paint a special presentation piece, but he delays five years—presumably because he is too busy and popular to worry much about the Academy. In the meantime he stays with a wealthy patron called Pierre Crozat, paints a set of *Seasons* (plate 11) for him, and gets his first really wide acquaintance with the Old Masters by studying Crozat's wonderful collection. The influence of Titian and other masters can be seen in Watteau's choice of mythological subjects (though hardly treated very seriously) and in his use of darker, richer tones (plates 12, 13).

Watteau had already achieved his mature style by the time he was ready to become a full member of the Academy. This happened in 1717, when he presented *The Embarkation for*

Cythera (plates 26, 27). The Academy recognised his distinctive subject matter by putting him down as 'painter of *fêtes galantes*', thereby creating a new category in the Academy records. Watteau had arrived.

The *Embarkation* remains Watteau's most famous picture, unique in its evocation of the mingled pleasures and regrets of all departures. Watteau seems to have been obsessed by the image of the pilgrim; it appears much earlier in his work in the literal form of a sturdy old man with the pilgrim's traditional staff, cockleshells and wallet (scrip). But now the pilgrims are lovers, perfunctorily equipped with staves, who are setting out for the island of love. Or rather that is where they should be going: all the evidence suggests that they are in fact on the island and about to leave it. After all, they have paired off, the day is drawing to its close, and—above all—the whole atmosphere suggests the ending rather than the beginning of an idyll.

It was quite typical of Watteau to take such liberties with his sources. For the *Embarkation*, like so much of his work, is taken from a theatrical performance—in this case one that can be named and dated. *The Three Cousins,* a piece by Florent Dancourt that was revived in Paris during 1709, has an episode in which girl pilgrims set off for Cythera in search of sweethearts. Watteau's much earlier version (plate 9) may very well be a faithful rendering of the performance, with its figures lined up in the foreground, and a background that has the slightly unconvincing quality of painted scenery. The version Watteau made for his friend Juillard (plate 29) is essentially a variation on the Academy *Embarkation*, but there are more figures and many subtle new touches that create an atmosphere that is lighter and more truly Rococo, though just for that reason a little less distinctive and distinguished. Cheery, mischievous cherubs and cupids are everywhere, and the presiding spirit of the scene is no longer an armless bust but a benign Venus and Cupid. Busts and statues turn up in most of Watteau's paintings, making their presence felt as sympathetic onlookers who might almost be tempted to participate. There is a quality about them that suggests mockery of conventional classical solemnity. In some later paintings (plates 35, 39, 40) they assume postures of erotic abandon that seem like comments on the refined attitudes of the human actors.

'Actors' seems the right word, for the theatre was Watteau's overriding obsession. As well as the various *Embarkations* the plates in this book include two pairs contrasting the Théâtre Francais and the Théâtre Italien (plates 22/23, 45/46). And in other pictures the action is often confined to the paved area of a building looking out on a countryside that might well be a backdrop (plates 20, 31); banded columns down each side of the painting complete the illusion—if illusion it is—that we are looking at a stage set.

The confusion between pictured reality and pictured illusion is made greater by the intrusion of fictional characters into the *fêtes galantes*, and of Watteau's friends into theatrical scenes. The fictional invaders are characters from the Théâtre Italien, which was obviously closer to Watteau's heart than the more formal Théâtre Francais, then already a bastion of the grand style. The Italian players performed the traditional repertoire of the *commedia dell'arte*, which involved improvising dialogue around stock situations and well known characters: star-crossed lovers, tyrannical fathers, avaricious old suitors, cowardly braggarts, simple-minded dupes, and resourceful rascally servants. From the Italian Comedy Watteau took not only characters but possibly even the costumes that comprise one of the chief idiosyncrasies of his pictures–vaguely 16th-century clothing that is worn with 18th-century negligence. (There is some doubt about the point since the company was banned from Paris until 1716, by which time Watteau had largely formed his style. But of course he may well have found out about the 'Italians' via prints or other means.)

Watteau draws very heavily on his sources, but he also transforms them. In *Harlequin and Columbine* (plate 21) the masked and chequered trickster and his soubrette sweetheart are drawn into the special mood of Watteau's world. The same is true of such pictures as *Love at the Théâtre Italien* (plate 23), which has little in common with the rapid, witty and often scurrilous performances of the company. Furthermore the characters that engaged Watteau's interest were neither the lovers nor the rogues, though they were the audience's favourites. He makes much of the minor character Mezzetino, the stripe-suited guitarist, who is lighting the stage by holding up a flare in plate 23. Watteau painted his friend, the dealer Sirois, as Mezzetino (plate 15), and also portrayed the character giving voice to a hopeless passion (plate 37)–a portrait all the more touching because of Mezzetino's rather unattractive, fleshy appearance. As so often in Watteau's paintings, the statue, her back firmly turned on Mezzetino, contributes to the action.

Watteau also transforms Pierrot (often called Gilles in France); he was one of the first people to feel compassion for this born loser who is the butt of every joke and the victim of cruel tricks. In *The Italian Players* (plate 46) Gilles, though apparently taking a curtain call, looks more like a saint exposed to a hostile crowd before being martyred. The picture was painted in 1720 for a Dr Mead, whom Watteau consulted in London about his tubercular condition. It is tempting to believe that Gilles is a real or imaginary 'portrait of the artist', alienated from the crowd through illness or vocation. The later *Gilles* (plate 47) cannot have been painted long before Watteau's death in 1721. The figure of Gilles is awkward and defenceless in his voluminous finery; the arms hanging limply in front of him and the sleeves creeping down his wrists emphasise his vulnerability. Gilles's face suggests a long-suffering beast of burden–far more so than the sentimentalised donkey in the picture, though the two were often equated in *commedia dell' arte* performances.

These paintings of Watteau's last years have a much greater definition and realism. Men and women begin to dominate the action instead of blending with the landscape in the interests of an overall mood. It looks as though Watteau was beginning to turn from lyric poetry (so to speak) to drama.

The most famous work of Watteau's last years is the shop-sign he painted for Edmé Gersaint's gallery (plate 44), which has unfortunately been cut in two. Watteau was staying with Gersaint and, though already gravely ill, insisted on painting the sign for his friend. He seems to have disliked feeling a sense of obligation, and he must have known that an eager buyer would soon induce Gersaint to part with the sign, as in fact happened. Many unusual features of the painting—Watteau's use of contemporary dress, the urban tones of brown, the atmosphere of relaxed activity—can be explained by its purpose: melancholy 16th-century figures in a landscape would hardly have made much impact as an advertisement. On the other hand Watteau was not the sort of artist who could go through with a really big project for which he had no natural inclination. So it seems likely that Gersaint's shopsign, along with the other works of 1720–21, represents a new departure by Watteau. Such evidences of change remind us that Watteau was only thirty seven when he died of tuberculosis, longing to go home to Valenciennes though too weak to be moved. Had he lived for another dozen years or more he would probably have developed an entirely new style and tackled entirely different subjects from those with which we are familiar. What we have are really only the early works of Watteau, splendid though they are; but with them we must be content.

THE PLATES

All pictures are oil on canvas unless otherwise stated.

1 *Singerie. c.* 1709. Plumbago and red chalk. $27\frac{1}{2} \times 19\frac{1}{2}$ in. (69.7×49.5 cm.). Nationalmuseum, Stockholm.

2 *The Cajoler.* 1708. Panel, $31\frac{1}{4} \times 15\frac{3}{8}$ in. (79.5×39 cm.). Cailleux Collection, Paris.

3 *The Faun. c.* 1708. Panel. $34\frac{1}{4} \times 15\frac{3}{8}$ in. (87×39 cm.). Cailleux Collection, Paris.

4 *A couple*, after Rubens. Red chalk. $9\frac{1}{4} \times 5\frac{3}{4}$ in. (23.3×14.7 cm.). Musée des Arts Décoratifs, Paris.

5 *The Pilgrim. c.* 1710. Red, black and white chalk on buff paper. $14\frac{5}{8} \times 9\frac{7}{8}$ in. (37.2×25.1 cm.). Musée du Petit Palais, Paris.

6 *Soldiers.* Red chalk. $7 \times 8\frac{1}{2}$ in. (17.4×21.8 cm.). École Nationale Supérieure des Beaux-Arts, Paris.

7 *The March Past. c.* 1709. $12\frac{3}{4} \times 17$ in. (32.4×43.2 cm.). City of York Art Gallery.

8 *The Village Bride.* $25\frac{1}{2} \times 36\frac{1}{4}$ in. (63×92 cm.). Sir John Soane's Museum, London.

9 *The Island of Cythera. c.* 1709. $17\frac{3}{4} \times 21\frac{3}{4}$ in. (46×55.5 cm.). Heugel Collection, Paris.

10 *The View.* $17\frac{3}{4} \times 21\frac{1}{2}$ in. (46.9×56.7 cm.). Courtesy Museum of Fine Arts, Boston. Marie Antoinette Evens Fund.

11 *Summer. c.* 1715. $54\frac{1}{2} \times 49\frac{1}{2}$ in. (138.5×125.8 cm.). National Gallery of Art, Washington D.C., Samuel Kress Collection.

12 *Love Disarmed. c.* 1715. $18\frac{1}{2} \times 15$ in. (47×38 cm.). Musée Condé, Chantilly.

13 *Jupiter and Antiope. c.* 1713. $28\frac{3}{8} \times 43\frac{1}{4}$ in. (72×110 cm.). Louvre, Paris.

14 *A Persian.* 1715. Red and black chalk, $9\frac{7}{8} \times 6\frac{1}{4}$ in. (25.1×15.7 cm.). Kunstverzamelingen, Teylers Stichting, Haarlem.

15 *Sirois and his Family.* $10\frac{3}{8} \times 7\frac{7}{8}$ in. (26×20 cm.). Wallace Collection, London.

16 *Young Woman with Lute. c.* 1716. $10\frac{1}{4} \times 7\frac{1}{2}$ in. (25×19 cm.). Louvre, Paris.

17 *Young Man Dancing. c.* 1716. $10\frac{3}{8} \times 8$ in. (26×20 cm.). Louvre, Paris

18 *Two studies of a Woman seated. c.* 1716. Red chalk. $8 \times 13\frac{3}{8}$ in. (20.2×34 cm.). Rijksmuseum, Amsterdam.

19 *Love Song. c.* 1715. $20 \times 23\frac{1}{2}$ in. (50.8×58.4 cm.). National Gallery, London.

20 *Bal Champêtre (Les Plaisirs du Bal).* $19\frac{3}{4} \times 24\frac{3}{8}$ in. (50×62 cm.). Dulwich College Gallery, London.

21 *Harlequin and Columbine.* $13\frac{1}{2} \times 10\frac{1}{2}$ in. (34.3×25.7 cm.). Wallace Collection, London.

22 *Love at the Théâtre Francais.* 1716? $14\frac{1}{2} \times 18\frac{7}{8}$ in. (37×48 cm.). Staatliche Museen, Gemäldegalerie Berlin-Dahlem.

23 *Love at the Théâtre Italien.* 1716? $14\frac{1}{2} \times 18\frac{7}{8}$ in. (37×48 cm.). Staatliche Museen, Gemäldegalerie Berlin-Dahlem.

24 *Gathering in a Park. c.* 1716. $12\frac{5}{8} \times 18\frac{1}{8}$ in. (32×46 cm.). Louvre, Paris.

25 *The Two Cousins.* 12×14 in. (29×35 cm.). Marquis de Ganay Collection, Paris.

26, 27 *Embarkation for Cythera*; and detail. 1717. $50 \times 75\frac{1}{2}$ in. (127×192 cm.). Louvre, Paris.

28 *Study for The Embarkation for Cythera.* Red, black and white chalks on buff paper. $13\frac{1}{4} \times 8\frac{7}{8}$ in. (33.6×22.6 cm.). British Museum, London.

29 *Embarkation for Cythera.* $50\frac{3}{4} \times 76\frac{3}{4}$ in. (130×192 cm.). Staatliche Museen, Gemäldegalerie Berlin-Dahlem.

30 *Three Studies of a Woman. c.* 1716. Black and red chalk and plumbago on buff paper. $9 \times 11\frac{1}{2}$ in. (23×29 cm.). Louvre, Paris.

31 *The Music Party.* $25\frac{1}{2} \times 36\frac{1}{4}$ in. (64.8×92.1 cm.). Wallace Collection, London.

32 *Study of a Negro. c.* 1716. Red and black chalk heightened with white on grey paper. $7\frac{1}{8} \times 5\frac{3}{4}$ in. (18×14.5 cm.). British Museum, London.

33 *The Concert.* 1716/17. $26 \times 34\frac{3}{4}$ in. (66×91 cm.). Verwaltung der Staatlichen Schlösser und Gärten, Charlottenburg-Berlin.

34 *Two Studies of a Bagpipe Player.* Red chalk with touches of black and white chalk. $11 \times 8\frac{1}{4}$ in. (28×21 cm.). Louvre, Paris.

35 *Les Fêtes Venitiennes.* $21\frac{1}{2} \times 17\frac{3}{4}$ in. (54.5×45 cm.). National Gallery of Scotland, Edinburgh.

36 *Nude Woman.* Red, black and white chalks. $9\frac{1}{16} \times 9\frac{1}{16}$ in. (23×23 cm.). Musée des Beaux-Arts, Lille.

37 *Mezzetino. c.* 1719. $21 \times 16\frac{3}{4}$ in. (53.5×42.5 cm.). Metropolitan Museum of Art, New York, Munsey Fund, 1934.

38, 39 *Champs Elysées*; and detail. *c.* 1719. $12\frac{1}{2} \times 16\frac{3}{8}$ in. (31.4 × 40.6 cm.). Wallace Collection, London.

40 *Fête in a Park. c.* 1720. 49 × 74 in. (125 × 188 cm.). Wallace Collection, London.

41 *The Halt during the Chase.* 1720. $48\frac{1}{2} \times 74$ in. (124 × 188 cm.). Wallace Collection, London.

42 *La Toilette. c.* 1720. $17\frac{1}{2} \times 14\frac{1}{4}$ in. (44 × 37 cm.). Wallace Collection, London.

43 *Judgement of Paris.* 1721? $18\frac{1}{2} \times 12\frac{1}{4}$ in. (47 × 31 cm.). Louvre, Paris.

44 *Gersaint's Shopsign.* 1721. $71\frac{3}{4} \times 121\frac{1}{4}$ in. (182 × 307 cm.). Staatliche Museen, Gemäldegalerie Berlin-Dahlem.

45 *Les Comédiens Français.* 1720. $22\frac{1}{2} \times 28\frac{3}{4}$ in. (47 × 73 cm.). Metropolitan Museum of Art, New York, Jules S. Bache Collection, 1949.

46 *The Italian Players.* 1720. $26\frac{1}{2} \times 31\frac{7}{8}$ in. (67.5 × 81 cm.). National Gallery of Art, Washington D.C., Samuel H. Kress Collection.

47 *Gilles. c.* 1721. $72\frac{3}{8} \times 58\frac{5}{8}$ in. (184 × 149 cm.). Louvre, Paris.

Acknowledgements
The following photographs were supplied by:
Dulwich College, London, 20;
Hamlyn Group Picture Library, 2, 3, 4, 5, 7, 8, 9, 15, 19, 21, 26, 27, 28, 31, 32, 35, 38, 39, 40, 41, 42;
Metropolitan Museum of Art, New York, 37, 45;
Museum of Fine Art, Boston, 10;
National Gallery of Art, Washington 11, 46;
Nationalmuseum, Stockholm, 1;
Photographie Giraudon, Paris, 6, 25, 36;
Rijksmuseum, Amsterdam, 18;
Staatliche Museen, Gemäldegalerie, Berlin–Dahlem, 22, 23, 44;
Walter Steinkoff, Berlin–Dahlem, 29, 33;
Studio Nico, Haarlem, 14;
André Held–Joseph P. Ziolo, Paris, 12, 13, 16, 17, 24, 30, 34, 43, 47.

1

2

4

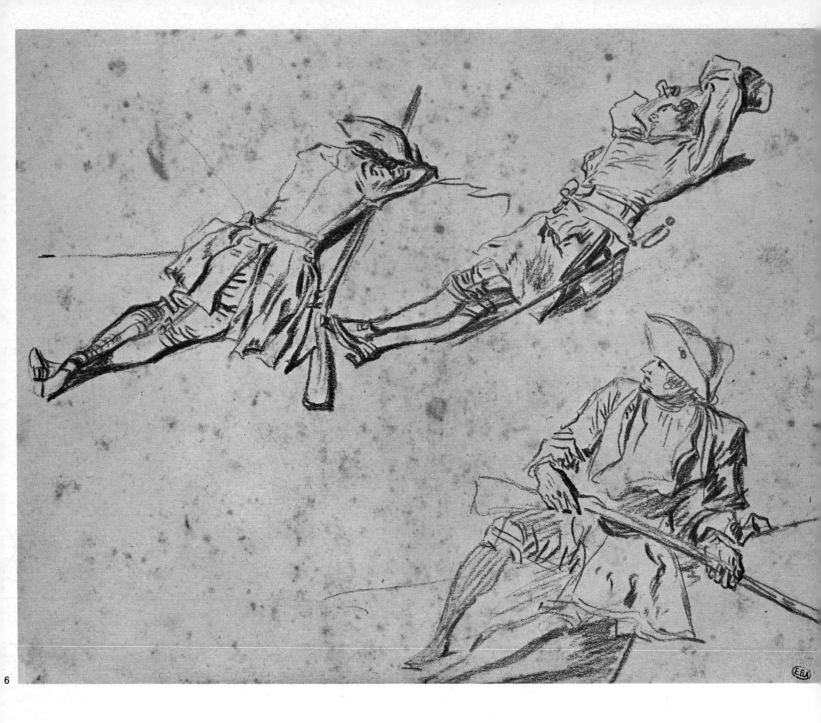

6

8

4

23

3

2

4

5

Canaletto

The Venetian painter Canaletto might be called the first great artist of place. In his hands, what had been a promising but minor type of picture attained rapid maturity in the 1720s and 1730s. The *veduta*, or view, offered an accurate record of an identifiable place, and offered it for its own sake. Palaces, squares and rivers were no longer to be painted exclusively as backgrounds, or else created in imaginary or drastically rearranged forms admired for their picturesqueness. The view satisfied the special 18th-century passion for reality and record – the passion that breaks out in the voluminous journals and memoirs of men such as Boswell and Casanova (himself a Venetian) Thanks to Canaletto, Venice was the chief beneficiary of the new trend, becoming the best visually documented of all 18th-century cities. Apart from the hundreds of paintings and drawings of Venice made by Canaletto himself, his achievement served to stimulate other Venetian artists such as Guardi and Longhi, who in turn made the city their special study.

Canaletto was born in Venice on 28 October 1697. His real name was Antonio Canal, and presumably he was called Canaletto ('little Canal') to distinguish him from his father Bernado, who was a painter of theatrical scenery. The nickname evidently stuck, and though Antonio never abandoned the name Canal (*da Canal* when he was flourishing his aristocratic pretensions), even he increasingly referred to himself as 'Canaletto'.

From at least the age of eighteen Canaletto was helping his father and his brother Cristoforo to paint scenery for Venetian theatres; among the productions on which he worked were two operas by Vivaldi. Scene painting was a skilled profession at this period. In Italy, 'legitimate' drama was an essentially aristocratic entertainment, and theatrical effects of all kinds were expected to be elaborate and spectacular. For the painter this meant covering flats and wings with heavily decorated imaginary buildings, and with streets, doorways and arcades down which a view stretched away to a distant horizon. As created by the Bibienas and other families of specialists, scene painting was an art of sumptuous illusionism.

It cannot have been easy for Canaletto to break with this tradition. One of his early biographers tells us that he decided to give up painting for the theatre in 1718, while he was on a trip to Rome with his father. If so, Canaletto failed to put his decision into effect, for he and Bernardo painted the scenery for two Scarlatti operas before returning to Venice. There he apparently joined the official fraternity of Venetian painters and had begun to emerge as an independent painter of views by 1722–23.

Within a very few years Canaletto had acquired an international reputation and an international clientele. Though there had been one or two view painters before him, they had produced nothing remotely comparable with his work of the 1720s and 1730s. Canaletto captured the unique quality of Venice's ancient yellowing stone and green waters. Less obviously, his designs are tremendously skilful, employing unusual and often daring viewpoints that enable the artist to create an effective work of art while remaining faithful to reality. Realism seems to have been increasingly important to Canaletto as he grew older. There is a lingering element of drama in the pictures of the 1720s, with their relatively dark tones and 'poetic' handling (for example plates 1, 14, 15). But by about 1730 Canaletto had arrived at his mature style, lighter and more clearcut–and so undramatic that the superficial viewer might mistake a painting such as the superbly designed *Grand Canal : Rialto* (plate 7) for a casual, unplanned 'photograph'. Canaletto's is an art that conceals art.

The Venice we see in his paintings, however, is only a small part of the city. Whole areas, particularly the squalid tenements, almost never appear, and brawny, healthy *gondolieri*–rather than the ragged and undernourished–generally represent the poorer classes. The reason for this lay in the market Canaletto worked for. His paintings were executed for the tourist trade. His customers were foreigners who wanted views of the famous sights of Venice. With these they could remind themselves of what they had seen on the Grand Tour or, in some cases, what they had missed but wanted to be able to talk about.

That is why the same landmarks occur again and again in Canaletto's pictures. He painted St Mark's and the Doge's Palace dozens of times, showing amazing ingenuity in the way that he varied the viewpoint and distance, so that even views painted for patrons in different countries are never identical. For us, one advantage of this limitation is that we can fairly easily get our bearings in Canaletto's Venice and relate one picture to another in geographical terms. St Mark's Square is of course the most famous spot in Venice, and views of the domed church of St Mark (San Marco) and the Campanile (bell tower) are found both early (plates 1, 2) and late (plates 47, 48) in Canaletto's career. The

'eastern' appearance of St Mark's, witnessing the long history of Venetian trade with Byzantium and the Levant, is equally noticeable in the richly decorated interior (plate 3). Viewing the square from a different angle–from the waterfront area called the Molo–the Campanile is now on the spectator's left and the facade of St Mark's is half hidden to the right (plate 4). Drawing back still further at almost the same angle (plate 5) we can now see the Molo with St Theodoric's column and the Doge's Palace in front of St Mark's. Another view is along the Molo, with St Theodoric's column on the right, towards the famous church of Santa Maria della Salute in the distance across the water (plate 6).

Once identified, the buildings mentioned so far can also be spotted in panoramic views such as plate 9, which shows the whole of St Mark's Basin from the Grand Canal. The canal is the main artery of Venice, and is the other main focus of Canaletto's paintings. One of the bridges across it is the famous Rialto (plates 7, 8), among whose shops and stalls the villainous Shylock is said in *The Merchant of Venice* to have made his deals and ducats.

Canaletto's Venice, stretching down the Grand Canal and along St Mark's Basin, can be seen in the course of a few minutes from one of the city's water-taxis. Of the landmarks not on this route, the best known is the church of SS Giovanni e Paolo (plate 14), which contains the tombs of many of the Doges. Outside, on the square, is Verrocchio's great statue of Bartolommeo Colleoni, a 15th-century mercenary soldier who faithfully served the Venetian Republic. In another painting (plate 25) Canaletto has made the statue itself the centre of his attention.

Many of Canaletto's paintings are devoted to great ceremonial occasions. These were one of the great tourist attractions of Venice—and all the more picturesque for being mere functionless survivals of a past glory. The most famous of all such occasions took place on Ascension Day, when the Doge was rowed out to sea in the state barge, the Bucintoro, and solemnly wed the sea by throwing a ring into it. The act symbolised the naval supremacy that had made Venice safe and rich—a supremacy that had long since passed. In the plate reproduced here (plate 21) the Bucintoro is just returning to the Molo after the ceremony.

Another annual occasion was the Doge's visit to the church of San Rocco (plates 11–13), commemorating the saint's protection of Venice against the plague of 1575. A relatively small part of the church is visible on the right. The building in the centre of the painting is the Scuola di San Rocco, which houses a great cycle of paintings by the 16th-century artist Tintoretto.

There were also four night festivals every year (plate 28) and regattas (plates 23, 24) at least once a year. The word regatta, incidentally, is Venetian in origin, like the word 'arsenal', which was the name of the famous shipyard, which had once been the greatest in Europe, capable of turning out a full-sized galley every day.

Canaletto worked on at the centre of this world, prosperous and famous, until the 1740s. Then times changed. In 1741 Frederick the Great of Prussia marched his troops into Silesia and triggered off the War of the Austrian Succession, which soon spread into Italy and the rest of Europe, lasting until 1748. 18th-century wars were relatively civilised affairs, but all the

same they discouraged tourism. Commissions for paintings from Canaletto seem to have fallen off, and we find him engaged in some uncharacteristic activities, presumably in an attempt to make ends meet. He ventured outside the city to paint views of Padua and other Venetian possessions on the mainland. He made a magnificent series of etchings (despite the fact that he had never done anything of the sort before). He also painted some views of Rome—probably without moving from Venice, but using drawings made in 1719–20.

Then, in 1746, Canaletto left Venice and went to work in England. This was a radical decision for a man approaching fifty who had not previously shown the slightest taste for travel. It looks as though times were still hard and Canaletto thought it advisable to go where he could remain in contact with his most reliable patrons. For England was the country where Canaletto was best known, and also the country with the wealthiest and most generous patrons of the arts. This was the age when the 'English milord' was the envy of Europe, enriched by commerce as well as his estates, but not yet swamped by the Industrial Revolution and the rising middle class. Probably the bulk of Canaletto's Venetian views had been produced for English customers. The Duke of Bedford, for example, had commissioned twenty four views (plates 20, 26–27), and the Duke of Richmond had purchased paintings by Canaletto through his agent, Owen McSwiney. But from the 1730s the dominant figure in Canaletto's working life was Joseph Smith, an English merchant who had been resident in Venice since the early years of the century. Smith built up a wonderful collection of Canalettos which he eventually sold to King George III; the fifty-odd paintings and almost one hundred and fifty drawings are still by far the largest and best collection of the artist's work anywhere in the world. Smith also acted as an intermediary between Canaletto and would-be buyers. According to one account the Italian was under exclusive contract to Smith, and their relationship was a stormy one. Smith certainly complained of Canaletto's 'impertinences' as McSwiney had done before him. But whether this was a sign of English arrogance or Italian temperament is impossible to decide at this distance in time.

At any rate, when Canaletto left Venice, Smith (who had recently become the city's English consul) furnished the painter with the necessary introductions. Canaletto stayed in England for the next ten years, making only two short trips back to Venice. He would hardly have stayed so long had he been received with hostility, so accounts of his failures in England are probably exaggerated. On the other hand it seems clear that the English *were* a bit disappointed. Canaletto's work was not quite so good as it had been in the 1720s. And with the painter working in England and painting familiar English things such as the brand-new Westminster Bridge (plates 34, 35) there was no question of age and distance lending enchantment. Most irritating of all to Englishmen—then and ever since—is the way in which Canaletto bathed all his scenes (plates 31–42) in a mellow Venetian light that is almost never seen in England. To appreciate them purely as paintings it is an advantage to forget that they are supposed to show England— and that of course is just what Canaletto's patrons were not prepared to do.

At one point word even got about that the Italian was an imposter posing as Canaletto. The painter was suspiciously secretive, for he always tried to avoid letting anyone see him at work. (Perhaps he realised that Englishmen might feel disillusioned when they saw him using mechanical aids such as the optic camera, which saved the painter a great deal of preparatory work by throwing a little image of the subject which the artist could trace.) Furthermore a 'Canaletto' was known to be working in Germany: perhaps he was the real master. In fact he was the painter's nephew, Bernardo Bellotto, who was also a view painter of great talent, and who exploited the family connection by using his uncle's nickname. The rumour was evidently serious enough to convince Canaletto that he should show one of his paintings to the public at large, and he put an advertisement to that effect in the newspapers.

In spite of everything that has been said, Canaletto's English paintings are never less than highly skilful, and are sometimes inspired. It is arguable whether he ever did anything better than *London seen through an Arch of Westminster Bridge* (plate 33), using the wooden supports (not yet knocked away from the newly built structure) as a daringly effective frame. Or than the cool, splendidly organised *Thames from Somerset House* (plate 32). Canaletto's patrons included great nobles for whom he painted some of the pictures reproduced in this book such as the Duke of Richmond (plate 31), the Duke of Northumberland (plates 33, 42), the Earl of Warwick (plate 40), the Duke of Beaufort (plate 41), and also a gentleman called Thomas Hollis (plate 39). Evidently he was not, in any meaningful sense of the word, a failure in England.

In 1756 Canaletto left England and returned to Venice for good. The last direct account of him dates from four years later, when two English travellers spotted him in St Mark's Square, still patiently sketching in preparation for a finished drawing or painting. In his last years Canaletto became a respected figure in Venice, finally overcoming all opposition (presumably on the part of conservatives who looked down on view painting) by being elected to the Academy of Painting and Sculpture (1763).

Following tradition, he celebrated the event by presenting the academy with a painting—in this case a capriccio (plate 46). A capriccio ('caprice') was a cross between a real view and pure architectural fantasy. It involved painting actual or near-realistic buildings in unlikely or imaginary settings. Two of Canaletto's capriccios (plates 43, 44) look as though they combine English and Italian elements, and may well have been painted in England. The capriccio was an exercise in ingenuity, challenging the painter to bring together disparate elements in an effective design with a coherent mood. Canaletto seems to have become more interested in the genre as he grew older, as if reverting to the grandiose tradition of scene painting in which he was brought up. The last of the Canalettos in this book—a pure architectural fantasy done with a pen and wash (plate 49)—is paradoxically the most theatrical.

Canaletto died in April 1768. He was working almost to the last, for there is a drawing by him that dates from only two years earlier. On it the artist has written his name and the fact that he had done the work 'at the age of sixty eight and without spectacles'.

THE PLATES

1, 2 *St Mark's Square*; and detail. *c.* 1723. Oil on canvas. 56 × 84¾ in. (142 × 205 cm.). Thyssen Bornemisza Collection, Lugano.

3 *Interior of St Mark's. c.* 1756? Oil on canvas. 16½ × 11½ in. (42 × 29 cm.). Museum of Fine Arts, Montreal.

4 *The Piazzetta, looking north. c.* 1727. Oil on canvas. 67 × 51 in. (170.2 × 129.5 cm.). Reproduced by gracious permission of Her Majesty the Queen.

5 *The Molo and Piazzetta seen from St Mark's Basin. c.* 1732. Oil on canvas. 18½ × 31 in. (47 × 78.8 cm.). From the Woburn Abbey Collection by kind permission of His Grace the Duke of Bedford.

6 *The Molo, looking west.* 1740s. Oil on canvas. 43½ × 73 in. (110.5 × 185.5 cm.). Senator Albertini Collection, Rome.

7, 8 *The Grand Canal : Rialto*; and detail. Oil on copper. 18 × 23 in. (46 × 58.5 cm.). From Goodwood House, by courtesy of the Trustees.

9, 10 *St Mark's Basin*; and detail. Canvas. 49½ × 80¼ in. (125 × 153 cm.). Courtesy Museum of Fine Arts, Boston. Abbott Lawrence Fund, Seth K. Sweetser Fund and Charles Edward French Fund.

11, 12, 13 *The Doge visiting the Church and Scuola di San Rocco*; and details. Canvas. 58 × 78½ in. (147 × 199 cm.). National Gallery, London.

14 *SS Giovanni e Paolo and the Scuola di San Marco.* 1726. Canvas. 36 × 53½ in. (91.5 × 136 cm.). Mrs Howard Pillow, Montreal.

15 *The Grand Canal, looking from Santa Maria della Carità towards St Mark's Basin.* 1726. Canvas. 35½ × 52½ in. (90 × 132 cm.). Mrs Howard Pillow, Montreal.

16, 17 *Grand Canal : 'The Stonemason's Yard'.* 1729/30? Canvas. 48¾ × 64⅛ in. (124 × 163 cm.). National Gallery, London.

18, 19 *Grand Canal looking towards the Salute*; and detail. *c.* 1723. Canvas. 56 × 80½ in. (142 × 214 cm.). Thyssen Bornemisza Collection, Lugano.

20 *Entrance to the Arsenal. c.* 1723. Canvas. 18½ × 31 in. (47 × 78.8 cm.). Duke of Bedford, Woburn Abbey, Buckinghamshire.

21 *The Bucintoro Returning to the Molo on Ascension Day.* Canvas. 22 × 39½ in. (56 × 100.5 cm.). Dulwich College Picture Gallery, London.

22 *The Molo : the Fonteghetto della Farina.* Canvas. 14½ × 20 in. (37 × 51 cm.). Courtesy Museum of Fine Arts, Boston. Anonymous Gift.

23, 24 *Regatta on the Grand Canal*; and detail. Canvas. 48 × 72 in. (121 × 183 cm.). National Gallery, London.

25 *SS Giovanni e Paolo and the Colleoni Monument.* Canvas. 16¼ × 13¼ in. (41 × 35.5 cm.). Private Collection.

26, 27 *Campo San Stefano*; and detail. *c.* 1732. Canvas. 18½ × 31½ in. (47 × 80 cm.). From the Woburn Abbey Collection by kind permission of His Grace, the Duke of Bedford.

28 *Night Festival at San Pietro di Castello.* Canvas. 46⅞ × 72⅞ in. (119 × 185 cm.). On loan to Staatliche Museen, Gemäldegalerie, Berlin-Dahlem.

29 *View of Dolo on the River Brenta.* 1740s. Canvas. 24 × 37½ in. (61 × 94.6 cm.). Ashmolean Museum, Oxford.

30 *Padua Prato della Valle.* Canvas. 15¾ × 34½ in. (40 × 87.5 cm.). Lord Brownlow, Grantham.

31 *London : The Thames and City seen from Richmond House. c.* 1747. Canvas. 41¾ × 46¼ in. (105 × 117.5 cm.). From Goodwood House by courtesy of the Trustees.

32 *London : The Thames seen from the Terrace of Somerset House, looking towards St Paul's* (detail). *c.* 1750. Canvas. 43 × 73 in. (106.5 × 185.5 cm.). Royal Collection, Windsor.

33 *London seen through an Arch of Westminster Bridge.* 1746. Canvas. 22½ × 37½ in. (57 × 95 cm.). Duke of Northumberland, Alnwick, Northumberland.

34, 35 *London : The Lord Mayor's Procession, the Thames at Westminster Bridge*; and detail. 1746/47. Canvas. 37¼ × 50¼ in. (96 × 137.5 cm.). Mr and Mrs Paul Mellon Collection, Washington D.C.

36, 37 *London : Whitehall and the Privy Garden*; and detail. Canvas. 46¾ × 93½ in. (118.5 × 273.5 cm.). Duke of Buccleuch and Queensberry, Selkirk.

38 *London : The Old Horse Guards seen from St James's Park. c.* 1749? Canvas. 48 × 98 in. (122 × 249 cm.). The Viscount Fitz Harris, Winchester.

39 *Old Walton Bridge.* 1754. Canvas. $18\frac{1}{4} \times 29\frac{1}{2}$ in. (46.5×75 cm.). Dulwich College Picture Gallery, London.

40 *Warwick Castle: the East Front from the Courtyard.* Canvas. $29\frac{1}{2} \times 48$ in. (75×122 cm.). By kind permission of Lord Brooke, Warwick Castle.

41 *View of Badminton House, seen from the Park. c.* 1748. Canvas. $33\frac{3}{4} \times 48$ in. (86×122 cm.). Duke of Beaufort, Badminton House, Gloucestershire.

42 *View of Alnwick Castle, Northumberland.* Canvas. $44\frac{1}{4} \times 55$ in. (113.5×139.5 cm.). Duke of Northumberland, Alnwick, Northumberland.

43 *Landscape Capriccio with Column. c.* 1754. Canvas. 52×42 in. (132×106.5 cm.). National Gallery of Art, Washington D.C. Gift of Mr Paul Mellon, on loan to American Embassy, London.

44 *Landscape Capriccio with Palace. c.* 1754. Canvas. 52×41 in. (132×104 cm.). National Gallery of Art, Washington D.C. Gift of Mr Paul Mellon, on loan to American Embassy, London.

45 *Capriccio: Palace with Clock Tower and Roman Arch.* Canvas. $39\frac{1}{2} \times 57\frac{1}{2}$ in. (100.5×146 cm.). Duke of Norfolk, Arundel, Sussex.

46 *Capriccio: Colonnade opening on to the Courtyard of a Palace.* 1763. Canvas. $51\frac{1}{2} \times 35\frac{1}{2}$ in. (131×93 cm.). Accademia, Venice.

47 *St Mark's Square, showing part of the Colonnade of the Procuratie Nuove.* Canvas. 18×14 in. (45×35 cm.). National Gallery, London.

48 *St Mark's Square seen from the north west corner.* Canvas. $18\frac{1}{4} \times 14\frac{3}{4}$ in. (46.5×38 cm.). National Gallery, London.

49 *Architectural Fantasy: Flight of Steps leading up to the Loggia of a Palace.* Pen and ink drawing with grey wash. $14\frac{3}{4} \times 20\frac{3}{4}$ in. (36.3×53.1 cm.). Reproduced by gracious permission of Her Majesty the Queen.

Acknowledgements
The following photographs were supplied by:
Ashmolean Museum, Oxford, 29;
Dulwich College, 21, 39;
Hamlyn Group Picture Library, 1, 2, 5, 6, 7, 8, 14, 15, 18, 19, 20, 23, 24, 25, 26, 27, 28, 30, 31, 33, 36, 37, 40, 41, 42, 43, 44, 45, 46, 47, 48;
The Earl of Malmesbury, 38;
Mr and Mrs Paul Mellon, Washington 34, 35;
Museum of Fine Art, Boston, Massachusetts, 9, 10, 22;
Museum of Fine Art, Montreal, 3;
National Gallery, London, 11, 12, 13, 16, 17;
Royal Collection, 4, 32, 49.

1

2

3

4

9

1

12

32

83

5

3

41

48

Cézanne

Paul Cézanne was the last of the 19th-century martyrs of art, and also the first of the moderns. Like Vincent van Gogh and Paul Gauguin he was doomed to endure neglect or abuse for years; but unlike them he became widely admired in his own lifetime. His historical importance can be summarised in a few words. More than any other individual, Cézanne is responsible for the modern conviction that a work of art is not just a copy of reality but an independent creation that exists in its own right. In this way he made possible most of the great movements in modern painting from Cubism to Pop Art. Leaving history aside, he is one of the great painters of all time, combining the brilliance of the colourist with the solid forms and clear structures usually associated with a more linear, less 'painterly' tradition.

Cézanne was born on 19 January 1839. His birthplace, Aix, was a quiet provincial town in the south of France, only a few miles from Marseille and the Mediterranean. This region, with its rocky landscapes and harsh light, became an enduring influence on Cézanne's life and art. He spent his formative years there, writing romantic poetry and wandering with his boyhood friends Baptistin Baille and Emile Zola, and he returned again and again when Paris and the painters of Paris tired or disappointed him. Almost the whole of Cézanne's life revolved round these two poles: Aix and its environs, and Paris and the surrounding Ile de France area.

But first came the decision that he was to be a painter. This was made after two years at Aix University, where Cézanne had been set to study law to prepare him for his father's banking business. For a long time he had attended sessions at Aix's free drawing academy, but his father had resolutely opposed his desire to give up the law and study painting in Paris. He may well have surrendered only because Cézanne, though a good scholar was obviously incompetent in the ordinary affairs of life. So, when he was twenty two, Cézanne set off to conquer Paris.

It proved the most disastrous of false starts: within a few months Cézanne was back in Aix, working in his father's office. The causes of the disaster were partly personal (Cézanne was neurotically irritable and shy) and partly artistic (the Parisian avant-garde upset his hitherto conventional ideas). But it was at this point that Cézanne began to show his capacity for persistence. He again began to spend his spare time in the drawing academy, and in 1862 he went back to Paris. He stayed there, with occasional trips to the south, for the next eight years.

Cézanne matured remarkably slowly, both as a painter and as a man. He was tied emotionally to his family, and he never escaped the domination of his father, a self-made man who must have found his strange, apparently weak son a terrible disappointment. It was only when he reached the age of thirty that Cézanne managed to enter into a successful relationship outside his family, with a girl called Hortense Fiquet. In 1870 they set up house together at l'Estaquet, not far from Marseille, so that Cezanne could avoid being called up to serve in the Franco-Prussian war; and in 1872, soon after their return to Paris, Hortense bore him a son, also called Paul, whom he idolised. Even so, Cézanne still went in fear of his father, concealing the very existence of his own family until years later. The situation was made worse by the fact that Cézanne lived on an allowance from his father until he was well into middle age–though it is arguable that his humiliating dependance was preferable to the near-starvation experienced by less well connected artists such as Van Gogh.

From the letters, poems and paintings of his early years, we can get some idea of the tremendous stresses within Cézanne's personality. He was passionate and timid, impulsive, irascible, and incredibly repressed. (He could not bear to be touched, and he found it impossibly upsetting to paint from nude models.) What held him together was his religious devotion to painting and the tremendous self-discipline he was able to impose upon himself.

These insights into Cézanne's character help us to understand the direction in which his art developed–from the romantic and expressive to ever greater control and organisation. For this reason, only his earlier paintings tell us much about him. Often their tones are dark and the subjects sinister or violent–a murder, a dwarfish painter friend, a still life with a skull (plate 2), a macabrely erotic *Temptation of St Anthony* (plate 3) which is already remarkable for the simplified features and distortions of the figures. In a painting like the *Head of an Old Man* (plate 1) the violence comes out in the way in which the paint has been laid on, with slashing strokes of the palette knife. Yet even at this stage there is a strong hint of the willed calm and solidity of later years. *The Black Clock* (plate 4) is Cézanne's first masterpiece in a type of painting he was to make his own: the still-life.

A Modern Olympia (plate 5) is a strange baring of Cézanne's erotic nerve. On one level it is a parody of Edouard Manet's *Olympia*, a revolutionary painting that was still recent enough to be controversial. Cézanne's version, introducing a balding lecher and executed with a sketchy technique and raw colours, had nothing much in common with the cool, chic, tight look of Manet's work, though it throws interesting sidelights on Cézanne himself at a point when the man was about to disappear into the artist.

A Modern Olympia was painted at about the same time as *The House of the Hanged Man* (plate 6), which in spite of its title is a light-drenched landscape in the Impressionist manner. The Impressionists were a group of young men whose paintings were revolutionising art during Cézanne's early years in Paris. Instead of working conventionally from sketches in their studios, they took their easels into the open air. They tried to capture the appearance of a landscape at a given moment in time, working rapidly with little dabs of pure colour to create the blur and shimmer of things seen under strong light. To the critics, Impressionist dabs resulted in daubs, and every Impressionist exhibition caused an uproar among critics and public alike.

At first, Cézanne was outside all this. He knew most of the Impressionists, and two of them, Claude Monet and Auguste Renoir, became his friends. But he only adopted the Impressionist technique from 1872, when he took Hortense and Paul to stay at Pontoise, a little town outside Paris where Camille Pissarro lived. Pissarro was the oldest of the Impressionists, and his nine years' seniority probably made his influence acceptable to the cantankerously independent Cézanne. The two men tramped the countryside together, often painting the same view, and it was from this time that landscape became one of Cézanne's chief concerns. Pissarro was an ideal mentor who respected Cézanne's individuality, with the result that Cézanne revered him ever afterwards and even at the end of his life referred to Pissarro as his master. They worked together intermittently for over two years, and there is no doubt that Cézanne's art was transformed in that time.

But he was not to remain an Impressionist for long. He admired the colour and life that Impressionism had introduced into painting, but he also wanted to achieve the firmness and weight found in the classic art of the past—to 'make of Impressionism something solid and durable, like the art of the museums', as he put it. Even in *The House of the Hanged Man* Cézanne has sacrificed much of the hazy brilliance characteristic of Impressionism in order to create a firmly defined structure. His paintings were shown at the first Impressionist Exhibition of 1874, and again in 1877, but were almost universally abused. More thin-skinned than his fellows, and conscious of growing differences with them, Cézanne virtually withdrew from the public artistic life of his time. He worked for much longer periods in the south, and when he came to Paris he avoided most of his old acquaintances. Within a few years he seemed almost completely forgotten, and some people affected to believe he was dead.

During these years of 'exile' Cézanne created his distinctive style. It was a long and exhausting struggle; he had never had much technical facility, and now that he was breaking new ground he painted and repainted, sometimes devoting dozens of sessions to a single painting. Occasionally he despaired and threw the canvas away or slashed it with his palette knife. But in general Cézanne the painter had none of the instability of Cézanne the man; art aroused and engrossed all his enormous will-power and capacity for endurance.

Cézanne was most original in his approach to landscape. He responded with fervour to what he saw, but his response went far beyond photographic realism. In a picture like *The Little Bridge, Mennency* (plate 20), everything is 'solid and durable, like the art of the museums'— even the reflections in the water. Patterns of visible brushstrokes and a further element of organisation, also striking in *Rocks at l'Estaque* (plate 17), for example. They emphasise the fact that the picture *is* a picture, with an authentic existence to which the actual bridge or rocks are irrelevant. Equally original is the absence of a focal point of interest: Cézanne gives every area on the picture surface the same kind of attention and emphasis. The cohesive, unifying element is colour; the green of foliage (for example) reappears—non-realistically—on a bridge or in a shadow, as part of a complex arrangement of colours that makes so many of Cézanne's paintings masterpieces of balance and harmony. The demands of the composition are always allowed to take precedence over any other consideration.

This virtuoso use of colour is even more marked in another type of painting in which Cézanne was a master: the still-life. Here the painter's control is absolute. He chooses what items he will include and arranges them as he pleases. Yet even so, Cézanne's restless search for harmony and balance led him to flout appearances: many objects in his still-lifes are shown from conflicting viewpoints, and in *Still-life with Fruit Basket* (plate 29) the front edge of the table, broken by the hanging cloth, is not a straight line. This magnificently satisfying picture amply proves Cézanne's conviction that painting has its own peculiar laws.

The human element plays only a limited role in Cézanne's art. He abolished it from his landscapes, and anecdote and 'human interest' disappear after *A Modern Olympia*. The closest he comes to it is in the *Harlequin* (plate 28) and *Card Players* (plate 32) series; but both are triumphs of harmonious composition rather than human warmth. If there are any real exceptions they are in the paintings of bathers done by Cézanne from time to time (plates 37, 46, 47). The theme clearly had some special emotional significance for him, and the series culminates in the wild, strange architectonics of the large late versions (plates 46, 47).

But the portrait is the typical human subject in Cézanne's paintings. In this genre too he was a perfectionist, subjecting his sitters to a hundred or more sessions, during which they were expected to remain motionless. Not surprisingly, his most frequent and patient sitters were his wife Hortense (forty portraits, including plates 14 and 31) and himself (thirty five, including plates 11 and 16). All this effort was hardly for the sake of realism, whether literal or psychological. The features of the sitter are progressively simplified, leading up to the mask-

like faces of the magnificent late portraits (plates 42, 43); in fact it is now something of a cliché that Cézanne painted people as if they were still-lifes, telling one sitter who dared to stretch his limbs that 'apples don't move!' The endless sittings were given over to striving for the ideal harmony that obsessed Cézanne–a harmony that could only be achieved, for example, by the repeated patches of green in *Boy in a Red Waistcoat* (plate 35), and the elongation of the right arm that gives the composition much of its strength. For Cézanne the work of art is an end in itself, an object of contemplation in its own right; it should not be judged by comparison with external reality. That was the mistake of the French critics of Cézanne's day, who thought that the broken line of the table and the boy's long arm were proofs of Cézanne's incompetence. On the other hand, once the right priorities are established, it is worth remarking that there *is* a relationship between Cézanne's created reality and our world. Cézanne is not an abstract artist in disguise–indeed, retrospectively his work could almost be called an implied criticism of abstraction, for part at least of its strength is that it plays upon–and is played upon by–our knowledge of landscapes, interiors and men. It has no more nameable 'emotion' than a piece of chamber music, but for all that it moves and changes us.

Outwardly Cézanne's later life was uneventful, the only important exception being the years 1885–86. In the summer of 1885 he had a brief, mysterious love affair that was serious enough to stop him working for a time–the only break in several decades of unremitting activity. Next year, as if in reaction to this last fling, he married Hortense and thereby legitimised the now fourteen-year-old Paul. The ceremony was probably undergone to pacify Cézanne's respectable family, for it made little difference to his domestic relations; in fact Hortense and Paul spent most of their time in Paris while Cézanne worked on in solitude in the south. A more decisive event was his breach with his boyhood friend Zola, the hero of whose novel *The Masterpiece* was an artist-failure who resembled Cézanne closely enough to give lasting offence. Finally, Cézanne's father died, relieving him at last of his humiliating financial dependence.

In another man's life such a period might have been crucial—might be justly described as a time of endings, and perhaps of new beginnings. For Cézanne, dedicated to an art with its own laws of development, it seems to have had no significance that is discernable in his work. The sale of the Jas de Bouffan, the family house in the country outside Aix, may have upset him more, for the house and its surroundings were among his favourite subjects (plates 22, 23).

In the 1890s Cézanne's genius began to be recognised at last. Younger painters wrote to him or visited him to pay homage, and his paintings started to find their way into exhibitions. Most important of all, he was taken up by the picture dealer Ambroise Vollard, who from 1895 put on several full scale Cézanne exhibitions. Fittingly, Cézanne made Vollard the subject of one of his most powerful portraits (plate 43). Difficult to the last, he not only accepted his belated recognition as no more than his due, but also tended to take every opportunity to express his contempt for other painters. But, as we should expect, he was humbler when measuring his work against his own high standards, contenting himself with writing to friends that he was 'making progress'.

Cézanne carried on working to the end, tramping about the countryside and setting up his easel in all weathers despite advancing age and diabetes. It was on one such expedition that he was caught out in a violent storm and contracted pneumonia. The next day, 22 October 1906, Cézanne died, a martyr of art to the last.

THE PLATES

1 *Head of an Old Man.* 1865–68. Canvas. $20 \times 18\frac{1}{2}$ in. (51×48 cm.). Louvre, Paris.

2 *Still-life, Skull and Candlestick.* 1865–67. Canvas. $18\frac{3}{4} \times 24\frac{3}{8}$ in. (47.5×62.5 cm.). Private collection, Switzerland.

3 *Temptation of St Anthony.* 1869–70. Canvas. $22\frac{1}{2} \times 30$ in. (57×76 cm.). Bührle Collection, Zürich.

4 *The Black Clock.* 1869–70. Canvas. $21\frac{3}{4} \times 28\frac{3}{4}$ in. (54×73 cm.). Louvre, Paris.

5 *A Modern Olympia.* 1872–73. Canvas. 18×21 in. (46×55 cm.). Louvre, Paris.

6 *House of the Hanged Man, Auvers.* 1873. Canvas. $21 \times 26\frac{1}{4}$ in. (55.5×66.5 cm.). Louvre, Paris.

7 *Auvers : Village Panorama.* 1873–75. Canvas. $25\frac{1}{2} \times 31\frac{3}{4}$ in. (65×81 cm.). Art Institute of Chicago. Mr and Mrs Lewis L. Coburn Memorial Collection.

8 *Dahlias in a Delft Vase.* 1873–75. Canvas. $28\frac{3}{4} \times 21\frac{1}{4}$ in. (73×81 cm.). Louvre, Paris.

9 *Portrait of Victor of Chocquet.* 1876–77. Canvas. 18×14 in. (45.5×35.5 cm.). Private Collection.

10 *Still-life with Apples and Biscuits.* c. 1877. Canvas. $14\frac{7}{8} \times 21\frac{1}{2}$ in. (38×55 cm.). Louvre, Salle de l'Orangerie, Paris.

11 *Self-portrait.* c. 1879. Canvas. $13\frac{3}{4} \times 10\frac{5}{8}$ in. (35×27 cm.). Tate Gallery, London.

12 *Auvers from Harmé Valley.* 1879–82. Canvas. $28\frac{3}{4} \times 36$ in. (73×92 cm.). Kunsthaus, Zürich on loan from Paulette Goddard Remarque.

13 *L'Estaque ; the Village and Sea.* 1879–83. Canvas. $20\frac{1}{2} \times 24\frac{3}{4}$ in. (52×63 cm.). Siegfried Rosengart Collection, Lucerne.

14 *The Lady with the Fan : Mme Cézanne.* 1879–82. Canvas. $36\frac{1}{4} \times 28\frac{3}{4}$ in. (92×73 cm.). Bührle Collection, Zürich.

15 *Poplars.* 1879–82. Canvas. $24\frac{3}{8} \times 30\frac{3}{4}$ in. (61.5×78 cm.). Louvre, Paris.

16 *Self-portrait.* c. 1880–81. Canvas. $10\frac{1}{4} \times 5\frac{7}{8}$ in. (26×15 cm.). Louvre, Paris.

17 *Rocks at L'Estaque.* 1882–85. Canvas. $28\frac{3}{4} \times 33\frac{3}{4}$ in. (73×91 cm.). Museum of Art, São Paulo.

18 *Mount Marseilleveyre.* 1882–85. Canvas. 20×24 in. (51×62 cm.). Private Collection, Switzerland.

19 *Bay of Marseilles seen from l'Estaque.* 1882–85. Canvas. $22\frac{3}{4} \times 28\frac{1}{4}$ in. (58×72 cm.). Louvre, Paris.

20 *The Little Bridge, Mennency.* 1882–85. Canvas. $23\frac{5}{8} \times 28\frac{5}{8}$ in. (60×73 cm.). Louvre, Paris.

21 *Still-life with Soup Tureen.* 1883–85 ? Canvas. $25\frac{1}{2} \times 32$ in. (65×81.5 cm.). Louvre, Paris.

22 *Jas de Bouffan.* 1882–85. Canvas. $23\frac{3}{4} \times 28\frac{3}{4}$ in. (60.5×73.5 cm.). National Gallery, Prague.

23 *Trees at the Jas de Bouffan.* 1885–87. Canvas. $25\frac{1}{2} \times 31\frac{1}{4}$ in. (64.5×79 cm.). Courtauld Institute Galleries, London.

24 *Blue Vase.* 1885–87. Canvas. $24 \times 19\frac{5}{8}$ in. (62×51 cm.). Louvre, Paris.

25 *Trees and Houses.* 1885–87. Canvas. $26\frac{3}{4} \times 36$ in. (68×92 cm.). Lehman Collection, New York.

26 *Mont Ste Victoire.* c. 1886–88. Canvas. $26 \times 35\frac{3}{4}$ in. (66×89.5 cm.). Courtauld Institute Galleries, London.

27 *Aix : Rocky Landscape.* c. 1887. Canvas. $25\frac{5}{8} \times 31\frac{7}{8}$ in. (65×81 cm.). National Gallery, London.

28 *Harlequin.* c. 1889. Canvas. $36 \times 25\frac{1}{2}$ in. (91×64.5 cm.). Private Collection.

29 *Still-life with Fruit Basket.* c. 1888–90. Canvas. $25\frac{1}{2} \times 32$ in. (91×64.5 cm.). Louvre, Paris.

30 *Pot of Flowers and Pears.* c. 1880–90. Canvas. $17\frac{3}{4} \times 21\frac{1}{4}$ in. (45×53.3 cm.). Courtauld Institute Galleries, London.

31 *Portrait of Mme Cézanne in Red.* c. 1890. Canvas. $35 \times 27\frac{1}{2}$ in. (89×70 cm.). Museum of Art, São Paulo.

32 *Card Players.* c. 1893. Canvas. $23\frac{1}{2} \times 28\frac{3}{4}$ in. (59.5×73 cm.). Courtauld Institute Galleries, London.

33 *Still-life with Water Jug.* c. 1892–93. $20\frac{7}{8} \times 28$ in. (53×71 cm.). Tate Gallery, London.

34 *Man Smoking a Pipe.* c. 1892. Canvas. $28\frac{3}{4} \times 23\frac{1}{2}$ in. (73×59.5 cm.). Courtauld Institute Galleries, London.

35 *Boy in a Red Waistcoat.* 1890–95. Canvas. 31×25 in. (79×64 cm.). Bührle Collection, Zürich.

36 *Vase of Tulips.* 1890–94. Canvas. $23\frac{1}{2} \times 16\frac{5}{8}$ in. (59.6×42.3 cm.). Art Institute of Chicago. Gift of Annie Swan Coburn to the Mr and Mrs Lewis L. Coburn Memorial Collection.

37 *The Bathers*. 1890–94. Canvas. $8\frac{1}{2} \times 12\frac{1}{2}$ in. (22×33 cm.). Louvre, Paris.

38 *Still-life with Plaster Cast. c.* 1895. Oil on paper on wood. $26\frac{1}{2} \times 22\frac{1}{2}$ in. (69.5×57 cm.). Courtauld Institute Galleries, London.

39 *Portrait of Joachim Gasquet*. 1896–97. Canvas. $25\frac{5}{8} \times 21\frac{1}{4}$ in. (65.6×54.4 cm.). National Gallery, Prague.

40 *The Clockmaker. c.* 1895–1900. Canvas. $36\frac{1}{2} \times 28\frac{3}{4}$ in. (92.5×73.5 cm.). Solomon R. Guggenheim Museum, New York.

41 *The Lake of Annecy. c.* 1896. Canvas. $25\frac{1}{2} \times 32$ in. (64.5×81 cm.). Courtauld Institute Galleries, London.

42 *Old Woman with Rosary. c.* 1897–98. Canvas. $31\frac{3}{4} \times 26\frac{3}{4}$ in. (81×65.5 cm.). National Gallery, London.

43 *Portrait of Ambroise Vollard*. 1899. Canvas. $39\frac{1}{2} \times 31\frac{1}{2}$ in. (100×81 cm.). Petit Palais Museum, Paris.

44 *Still-life with Apples and Oranges*. 1896–1900. Canvas. $28\frac{3}{4} \times 36\frac{1}{2}$ in. (73×93 cm.). Louvre, Paris.

45 *Mont Ste-Victoire*. 1904. Canvas. $27\frac{1}{2} \times 35\frac{1}{4}$ in. (70×90 cm.). Philadelphia Museum of Art, Pennsylvania. George W. Elkins Collection.

46 *The Large Bathers*. 1898–1906. Canvas. $82 \times 98\frac{1}{4}$ in. (208×249.5 cm.). Museum of Art, Philadelphia.

47 *Les Grandes Baigneuses*. 1898–1906. Canvas. $50\frac{1}{8} \times 77\frac{1}{8}$ in. (127×195 cm.). National Gallery, London.

48 *The Gardener. c.* 1906. Canvas. $25\frac{3}{4} \times 21\frac{5}{8}$ in. (65.5×55 cm.). Tate Gallery, London.

Acknowledgements
The following photographs were supplied by:
Art Institute of Chicago, 7, 36;
Courtauld Institute Galleries, London, 26, 30, 34, 38, 41;
Solomon R. Guggenheim Museum, New York, 40;
Hamlyn Group Picture Library, 1, 2, 3, 8, 9, 11, 12, 13, 14, 17, 19, 21, 22, 23, 28, 29, 32, 33, 37, 39, 42, 44, 45, 46, 48;

Hans Hinz, Basle, 35;
National Gallery, London, 27, 47;
Photographie Giraudon, Paris, 4, 5, 15, 18, 25, 31, 43;
Scala, Antella, 10, 16, 20, 24;
Andre Held–Joseph P. Ziolo, Paris, 6.

2

3

4

2

1

2

4

4

1265